My Training Starts Tomorrow

The Everyman's Guide to IRONFIT
Swimming, Cycling, & Running

by
Roman Mica
3rd Edition

This book began life as a blog that chronicled my road to from Newbie to Ironman.

www.EverymanTriathlon.com is the honest chronicle of my continuing quest to find the deepest valleys and scale the highest peaks in the twisting road to endurance sport nirvana.

Heather Hummel (Ramsey), Editor

Cover Design by Randy Fredner
Photography by Roman Mica

PathBinder Publishing, LLC
Charlottesville, VA

My Training Starts Tomorrow
The Everyman's Guide to IRONFIT
Swimming, Cycling, & Running
3rd Edition

Cover Design: Randy Fredner
Photography: Roman Mica

ISBN: 0-9776232-0-3

Publisher:
PathBinder Publishing, LLC
P.O. Box 302
Earlysville, VA 22936
www.PathBinder.com

Acknowledgments

This book is dedicated to all the IronSherpas in my life that have given me the strength and support to compete in endurance sports.

I want to especially thank my beautiful wife and son, who are always ready and eager for a family race adventure. They have stood by me at the best of times and helped me through the worst of times. Without their love, friendship and warm morning smiles, I'd never be able to make it through the day. To my mother and stepfather whose support and love make it possible for us to live our active lives. To all of my friends and neighbors who think we're a bit crazy but encourage us all the same.

A special thank you must go to Heather Ramsey for her hard work in taking my random musing and making something great out of them.

And finally, I want to thank all of my readers who make up this great Everyman endurance community. I really enjoy talking with you during those long marathons and triathlons. Thank you all for your incredibly warm words of support and encouragement. Let's try to keep this crazy lifestyle our secret, as it surely is a great way to be alive.

Contents

Continued...

Contents (continued)

1
Newbie Mistakes

Top Ten Newbie Mistakes

In the military there's a saying that all the action happens at the tip of the spear; the sharply pointed end where the winners and losers are sorted out. For us newbie and amateur Clydesdale triathletes, the tip of the race is only a distant skirmish. We live and race at the other end of the spear; the round curvy end, which, as it happens, tends to be shaped like many of us. They say the best way to learn is to make mistakes. As a newbie and Clydesdale in my first year of competing, I've made my share of mistakes.

Here is my Top Ten List of Newbie Mistakes:

10) Wearing a black swim cap On the face of it, this one might seem a bit silly, but it's true.

"You're not gonna wear that black swim cap," the guy standing in the water next to me at the start solemnly said.

"I was planning on it," I replied, a bit confused.

"You don't want to do that," he added with a knowing nod.

"Why?" I asked a bit wide-eyed.

"Because they won't see go down when you drown," he added and swam away.

I looked into the dark murky water where he had been standing and considers this, removed the cap, and threw it to the shore. Only after the race did I remembered and reminded myself that I have dark hair.

9) Butt burn...otherwise known as the Lack-O-Glide factor. It took me about a year to discover the joys of lubrication. The leg pain after a marathon is nothing compared to the searing pain of taking a shower with raw nipples. However, nothing identifies a newbie triathlete like the Charlie Chaplin butt-burn-wobble-walk after an especially long bike session.

8) The Clydesdale category I'm a big guy at 6'2" and well over 200 pounds. I've always considered myself big in a gladiator sort of way. But according to the official rules, I'm big in a huge, wide-butted, beer wagon-pulling sort of way.

7) MAX, ADE, OX, GU, BOOM, GEL   There is a bewildering amount of performance enhancing drinks and supplements on the market. They have one thing in common: a fluorescent Day-Glo color. I tend to judge them by the stickiness factor. The more they make my hands stick to the handlebars of my bike, the better they must be.

6) Transitions are *not* free time For all of the pros out there, transitions may be free time. But for newbies, they are a time of profound confusion and terror. Mistakes happen all the time. "Why am I wearing my swim goggles?" I think as I power out of the transition area on my bike.

5) A wetsuit will kill   Try to remember to Valero the wetsuit zipper pull leash to your wetsuit. I didn't know I was supposed to attach the leash to the wetsuit the first time I wore it. About five minutes into the swim the leash wrapped itself around my neck like a viscous python bent on my death. The more I struggled to disengage myself from its death-like grip, the tighter it got. My flailing only seemed to encourage it. I finally did manage to free my throat and continue the swim. Five minutes later, it was back.

4) Big girls on mountain bikes Big girls on mountain bikes are surpassingly fast. Do not take it for granted that just because you are on a big ring, carbon fiber, aero bar out-fitted, race-tuned tri-bike that you'll easily pass that big girl up ahead. Make this mistake at your own peril and your self-esteem will suffer.

3) Du vs. Tri Don't confuse a duathlon with a triathlon when racing or checking the results. My first Olympic distance Tri was almost my last. I watched the awards ceremony with a mixture of terror and awe as the results and blazingly fast times were read out. I was amazed at the speedy results. Needless to say I was not the slowest triathlete in the world....just the only one at the duathlon awards ceremony.

2) Twelve year-old-lap counters When competing in a pool, avoid the twelve-year-old lap counter kids. I wondered out loud to one, "Why do I have to swim two more laps when the other two racers in my lane are done?" This seemed especially odd since "I had lapped both of them." The twelve-year-old was not moved by my logic. Math must not have been his best subject in school.

1) Beer Avoid all triathlons that are not sponsored by a brewery. Not only does a post race beer greatly help in the recovery process, but it also helps one forget all the mistakes. Plus as an added benefit after enough beers is now that big girl on the mountain bike doesn't seem so big.

2
My First Race

Don't Forget a Towel, for God's Sake!

I didn't think that a "Sprint" triathlon consisting of a 500-meter swim, a 15-mile bike ride, and a 4-mile run would be a big deal, but boy was I wrong.

I showed up early at the start of the Louisville Legacy Triathlon. I had my mountain bike, three sets of clothes (one for swimming, one for biking, one for running), two water bottles filled with warm water, a funky old helmet (the white egg shell with the orange stripes you sometimes see old guys still wearing), and my new expensive glass Revo sunglasses, which I purchased just for the race. I thought they made me look cool.

I was immediately struck by my first problem: where to rack my bike? Just for the record for all of the newbies reading this, the best answer is as close to the bike exit as possible. This way you don't have far to run in your bike shoes.

Of course I didn't know this. I also didn't know that you can rack your bike pointing outwards, thus making it much easier and faster to get the bike out during the race. But most of all I didn't know I needed a towel. Most other racers had towels, but I thought they were just for keeping their stuff clean while it was on the ground.

The first real "issue" was encountered before the start of the race. What to wear during the swim? I was smart enough to know that I couldn't change my shorts between the swim and the bike. I figured I had a decision to make. Swim in my bike shorts or bike in my swim shorts. I chose to swim in my bike shorts.

The error of this choice became immediately apparent when I jumped in and the fluffy bike short chamois sucked up about half the water in the pool. I was wearing something that now not only looked, but also felt, like a huge black swollen baby diaper. The shorts acted like a cruise ship anchor; slowing me way down while at the same time trying to **a)** pull me under and **b)** come off. The good news was that this in no way actually slowed me down because by the end of the first lap I was breathing so hard that I could barely swim at all.

Let's talk about training for a second. I had spent almost a full month getting ready for this race. And by a full month I mean I ran three miles about a half a dozen times, went mountain biking a few times, and swam once at a local recreation center for some unknown distance, which I only hoped was at least ten laps the length of the swim in the race.

Now I was on lap two out of ten and had switched from freestyle to the IM. Of course I didn't know what an IM was, but I was about to invent my own IM. As the saying goes, an IM in swimming is usually, "Fly, Back, Breast, Free, that's the way it's got to be." My own saying went something like this, "Free, Back, Angel, Breath, that's the way I won't heave."

By lap five I was almost reduced to walking, which I would have considered strongly had my legs actually been 15 feet long (the depth of the deep end of the pool). Instead, I switched to my mother's favorite stroke: the breaststroke. And I swam it just like her - with my head above the water. She does this to keep her hair dry. I did it to have unfettered access to air. Also the breaststroke enabled me to do the "froggy kick," which also happened to be the only kick that kept my swollen diaper shorts from sinking down to my ankles!

After what seemed like an eternity, I received the "last lap" signal and finished the swim. I jumped out of the pool, taking half of the water with me. I wish I could say that I ran to the transition area, but it was much more of a waddle, as I was out of breath, dizzy, and a bit disoriented.

It was in this semi-lucid state of mind that I wandered over to the transition area and immediately figured out why I needed a towel. My plan had been a simple one. I would just throw on my biking jersey and running shoes then head out for the bike. (I had no notion of biking clips.) I immediately ran into trouble. My wet and now dirty feet made it almost impossible to get my socks on. After the proper amount of jumping on one foot, strenuous tugging, and swearing, I managed to get the socks on over my wet feet.

By this point I was bright red from the lack of air and the epic struggle with the socks. On the verge of passing out, I went for the biking jersey. You have to know that in the best of situations, a typical biking jersey fits rather tightly on me. Back then, truth be told, I looked like a huge swollen yellow sausage bee in my "cool" tour jersey…even at the best of times.

This was not the best of times. The friction caused by my wet and chubby skin to succeed in halting the jersey about halfway down my stomach, and no amount of profuse tugging or swearing would get it down further. It was stuck somewhere above my belly but below my nipples. Now with the just half-on yellow jersey covering the top part of my body, and the swollen black diaper bike shorts covering the lower half, I really did look like a huge fat yellow sausage bee with a bright red pimple head.

What to do next? I plopped down on the ground and did what any experienced age-grouper would do in a similar situation. I stole my neighbor's towel. Okay, I didn't really steal it, I just borrowed it, and it did the trick. With dry skin, I was able to pull down the jersey and continue the race. I was a "cool" triathlete again. I was back in the race and feeling better.

The swim was over and I was heading out for a "short" 15-mile bike ride. I quickly grabbed my old-school helmet and threw it on my head. Naturally, I had completely forgotten that I had left my sunglasses in my helmet. This had seemed like such a good place to leave them earlier in the morning. As I threw the helmet on, the new Revos sailed through the air, over my head, over the next rack, and onto the cement ground. They hit the only way possible for expensive glass sunglasses to hit, that being glass first, and shattered.

I didn't know it back then, but I had just learned three very important lessons.

1) Train like you race. In other words, don't try anything new like swimming in bike shorts, and...
2) Find a better place for your sunglasses. Today I put them on my water bottle holder by inserting one leg between the water bottle and holder. I don't even touch them until I'm well into the bike. The less you have to worry about in the first transition the better, and...
3) Don't forget a towel — for God's Sake.

There is No Such Thing as a Sprint Triathlon

If you think about it, there is no such thing as a sprint triathlon. Triathlon is an endurance sport…one of the longest and hardest that tests an athlete's muscles, athletic abilities, mental toughness, strengths and weaknesses, and most importantly, endurance.

However, I suppose you could design a true sprint triathlon. It would look something like this:

1) A fifty meter freestyle swim
2) One lap around a Velodrome
3) A 100 meter dash

Now that would certainly be a Triathlon where transitions matter. I have not seen many Velodromes with indoor pools around my neck of the woods, so I wonder if this true Sprint Triathlon would have a hard time catching on. In America, the founding home of triathlon, if there is the will (and there's money to be made), there certainly will be a way.

For all you wannabe race directors, please feel free to take my true Sprint Triathlon idea and run with it. Just think of all the commercial possibilities for new true sprint triathlon gear. An entire new set of racing stuff we would buy to speed up the all-important transitions like:

- The Aqua Helmet
- The Running Goggle
- Nike's new full-body, one-piece, super fast-dry Shark/Lance/ Sprint skin complete Air racing cocoon leotard featuring built-in earplugs and built-in biking/sprinting cleats.

- Full "Body Glide Spray in a Can" to be able to remove Nike's new Air cocoon after a race.
- The GU Power Pellet for a super small and super fast burst of energy.
- The Nose Marker for marking the nose, which as it happens, is the only part of the body left exposed by the Nike's new Air Cocoon.
- Breathable and brimmed swim cap.
- IMskorts (swimming skirt and shorts).

A true sprint triathlon would also benefit completely different body types. Most of the current pros would have a hard time succeeding in this event. Let's face it, the ideal body type for a good or great triathlete is that of a depression era Nebraskan farmer.

I'm lucky enough to have met some pros up close and personal and to say these guys and gals have body fat would be like saying that Oprah has a hard time promoting herself. Unfortunately, when I started in this sport I misunderstood my goal for the ideal body. I've spent years trying to cultivate that perfect washtub stomach when all along I was supposed to have a washboard stomach. Oops!

Lets face it; one of the reasons so many of us Everyman Triathletes have taken up the sport is to lose weight. I know that my goal is to be fit (read: thin), enjoy a healthy lifestyle (read: eat whatever I like), and indulge in some friendly age-group competition (read: crush the other big guy with a 40 on his calf like a hapless bug).

For this reason, a true sprint triathlon would not really appeal to as many people, unless Dairy Queen created the nutritional race supplements. I'd call it the DQ Oreo Wizard for its magic ability to provide tons of calories while being smooth and delicious. Mmmmm…the DQ Oreo Wizard!

True sprinters (100 meters types) have bodies like Superman, not depression era Nebraskan farmers. These athletes have muscles from their toes to their ears. If I followed their high calorie/high strength work out training regime, my abs would go from being a washtub to a wash hot tub. Mmmmm…the DQ Oreo Wizard would make a great supplement, a short lift, and long hot tub.

Which brings me to the Super Ironman. Do you suppose it would be possible to train a world-class marathon runner (talk about depression era farmers body type) to be a world-class winning triathlete…The Super Ironman?

Now I know this may sound a bit silly, but when you consider it, this does seem to be possible. Arguably, the marathon runner is currently the ultimate world-class endurance athlete. Wouldn't he or she make the ultimate Super Ironman?

The men's world record marathon time currently stands around 2:05 and change. No pro has yet broken a 2:40 run in an Ironman. That's a 35-minute difference. This is an eternity at the professional level. The real question is, would it be possible to train a world-class runner to swim and bike fast enough to become the Super Ironman and still crush the current crop of pros like so many hapless bugs?

I think the swim part is certainly doable. Most current pros race the swim leg of an Ironman in about 55 minutes. We all know that runners usually make the worst swimmers, but I'm almost positive that even a great runner could get good enough to complete the swim in about one hour. That still leaves him with 30 minutes advantage on the run.

The better follow-up question would be, could a great runner stay within 10 minutes on the bike and still put down a 2:20 run to take the tape? I'm betting they could. Why? Because if you take a look at Lance, or any of the other top biking boys, they certainly look like marathon runners…okay, marathon runners with huge thighs.

Which brings me back to why there's no such thing as a true sprint triathlon. Many of us Everyman Triathletes started at the sprint level of the sport. I remember saying to myself before my very first race, "Self, why not sign-up for the Louisville Triathlon? After all, it is just a sprint tri?" It took me until the first transition to really understand what I had gotten myself into. I was about 10 minutes into the race; the swim was only 500 meters in a pool, but I was breathing harder at that first transition than I had ever breathed in my life. And yet I still had a 15-mile bike and 4.5 mile run to finish. I somehow managed to muddle my way through the bike (washtub stomach and all), while being passed by spry 84-year-olds on mountain bikes with massive under inflated knobby tires. On the run, my thighs seized up like the jaws of an angry alligator.

I kind of stumbled through the finish after having walked most of the "run." But I finished and I was a triathlete. I may never be a Super Ironman, but I finished the race in just over two hours, which by anybody's reckoning, is not a sprint.

3
Swimming is Fun!

Why the Swim is First

Have you ever spoken with a friend or acquaintance that has no knowledge of triathlon? I have, and I'm always amazed that they assume that the swim is last. It does seem logical that after all the biking, running, and sweating that swimming would be a great way to end the race.

The funny thing is that the history of triathlon proves that your friends are correct to put the swim last. This is from the USA Triathlon web site:

"1904 - An event in the Olympic Games was called triathlon, consisting of the long jump, shot put and 100-yard dash.

September 4, 1921 – The Petit Perillon swim club in Marseilles, France held an event called Course Des Trois Sports: The Race of Three Sports. The race consisted of a bicycle leg of about 7k, a run of 5k, and finished with a 200m out-and-back swim, and was won by Lulu Helmet.

1972 - David Pain, celebrating his 50th birthday, held a run-bike biathlon in San Diego, Calif., the first known multi-sport event in the United States.

September 1974 – While advertising its new race, the San Diego Track Club Newsletter headline read, 'Run, Cycle, Swim – Triathlon set for 25th,' using the word 'triathlon' for the first time in the modern sense.

January 1977 – John Collins challenged those gathered at the Oahu Perimeter Relay Run awards ceremony to compete in the first Iron Man Triathlon, a 2.4-mile swim, 112-mile bike, and 26.2-mile run.

February 18, 1978 – Fifteen men started and twelve men finished the first Ironman Triathlon, won by Gordon Haller in 11 hours 46 minutes 58 seconds."

You'll notice that it wasn't until the first Ironman in 1977 that the swim came was first. It is now common knowledge among triathletes that in such a long race there would be a much higher rate of drowning if the swim were last. Even in a wet-suit, it would be hard to walk the swim.

There are some other pretty interesting facts about the history of triathlon that jumped out at me. Can you guess what they might be?

1) The modern sport of triathlon really began at the Iron distance. You might think it would have been the Olympic distance that started it all, but it was the Iron Distance that really caught on first. This leaves me wondering why the Olympics doesn't have an Iron Distance race, and why is the International Long Course distance (4 kilometer swim, 120 kilometer bike, and 30 kilometer run) different from the Iron Distance?

Why are there so many different race distances?

There are at least 6:

1) Sprint
2) Olympic
3) Half Iron
4) International Long Course
5) Iron Distance (The Ironman)
6) Ultra Distance (The Ironman x 2)

Most other Olympic sports have one or two distances that are considered to be the standard. In running there are the 100-yard/meter dashes and the marathon. In swimming there are the 50-yard/meter freestyle sprints and perhaps the 200 IM. In biking it is the Tour de France, and don't ask me why. I suspect the French are somehow to blame. They did put on the first triathlon after all.

In triathlon we have at least half a dozen different distances that are considered to be a sprint. It's all very confusing to those of us who follow the sport, let alone the average Joe.

2) The next interesting fact that the history of triathlon shows is that it was an all boys sport, and I'll bet I know why. Most women are usually too busy and responsible to be sitting around Hawaii discussing which athletes are the most fit. "Is it a swimmer, a biker or a runner? Hard to say gentlemen, so let's find out by putting on a race that combines all three sports and let's make it...shall we say...a tad over 140 miles long."

There are several true and funny stories from the beginning years of the Ironman. During the first few years some of the racers would stop at a local restaurant, sit down, and order a nice meal during the race. Indeed one guy showed up with his bike loaded with food and camping equipment as he assumed it was a multi day event.

3) The most interesting fact is that triathlon is still a very young sport. For me, that's what makes it so great. The Pros don't yet make crazy amounts of money. It has not been commercialized, popularized, materialized, and sanitized. It is still a citizen's sport where you can hit the water next to some of the best in the world.

But most importantly, there's a small and rabid group of athletes who race and follow the sport while the rest of the world
wonders why we do such crazy things as swim, bike, and run
in one race. Shhhh, let's keep in our little secret. There's no
need to explain too much....and yes, the swim is last and that's
why all your friends should consider taking up the much safer
sport of golf.

The Hardest Start of Them All

I've been lucky enough throughout my sporting life to compete in a number of different sporting events. In college I both rowed and skied for my school. I also raced bikes on a local team and competed in both golf and tennis. I'll never forget the day my tennis career ended before it really began. I was in my last year of high school when my coach finally stated the obvious (after too many years of private lessons and summer tennis camps). "Let's face it Roman," he said, as I plucked at the strings of my tennis racket, "you're no Gazelle out there."

I'll also never forget what it felt like just before the start of my various sporting events. By far the easiest was a tennis match. Those you sort of ease into. There's not much pressure, as the first or fifth or fifteenth serve will not determine the outcome of the match. And if you fault, you always get a do-over serve to make up for the one you just screwed up.

On the other end of the pressure spectrum is the start of a slalom ski race. You only get one chance to get it right. You stand in the little hut freezing and shaking and staring down the course at the dizzying labyrinth of colorful gates. You know that the next 90 seconds will determine whether or not you just wasted the last 90 days of training. Your entire day, week, month is compressed to about the time it takes you to blink, for a blink will be the margin between the first and last place. You are keenly aware of this as you stare down the course. You wonder how you can shave a half a blink from your best possible time without catching an edge, blowing out of the course, or blowing out your knee.

The start of regatta is something completely different. I used to row in a heavy weight eight-man shell. We spent hours practicing the start of the race, as it often determines the end of the race. The start of this race is all about teamwork. You and seven other big guys have to work as one seamless unit. The eight oars have to catch and release the water at the exact same time while keeping the boat perfectly set-up. This means you have to keep the racing shell balanced on the equivalent of a knife's edge, as they do not balance themselves in the water like your typical boat. In fact, without the oars a racing shell would more likely than not flip over.

When you get the start right, the boat practically leaps out of the water as all eight men strain with their quads to rocket forward. With every stroke the shell surges ahead like a sixties muscle car on a weekend stoplight drag race, except the engine burning rubber is you and eight other guys working in perfect harmony to make this start happen.

When you get it wrong, one of the boys will catch a crab. This means, in non-rowing lingo, his oar gets stuck in the water as the boat surges ahead. The entire boat shudders as if you've just hit the emergency brake. The guy who caught the crab can be knocked unconscious and/or knocked out of the boat by the caught oar as it tries to sweep past his body.

The start of any longer running endurance race is a pretty casual affair. The gun goes off, I click my stopwatch, and I try to pace myself during the first mile or two until my body gets used to running. Depending on how I feel, I'll make this day one of my best, or sometimes one of my worst, race days.

But the start of a triathlon for me has always been the hardest start, for it consists of a moment that embodies a lifetime of sheer fear and unholy terror. In all the starts, in all the various races, I have never felt more scared or close to death as during the first five minutes of any triathlon. And the real kick in the ass is that I'm not afraid of the swim. In fact, it's probably the best part of my race. I don't come from a swimming background, yet I seem to take to it naturally, and I spend ample time in the pool swimming laps. But all this is completely irrelevant when I start the swim in a race because within about the first two minutes I think that on this day I will drown. There's something terrible that happens to me that I simply can't control, and I believe this something resembles the ancient fight or flight response.

I start the swim full of confidence and bravado. I don't hang back, and I'm not all that bothered by somebody swimming around, under, or over me. I don't even worry about getting kicked in the face or other more sensitive parts of my body. This part of the start is all good.

The part that is all bad is about two minutes into the race when I begin to hyperventilate. At first I only notice my heart beating as if it's trying to explode in my chest. Next I start to breathe harder and harder, which causes dizziness, and for the first time I realize that I'm actually thinking about drowning. This always comes as a complete surprise since I never think about drowning in the pool. At first I think to myself that this is silly and that I have to keep swimming, except that I can't seem to get enough air. I start gasping and gulping for air like a dying bass flopping around on the floor of a bass boat. I have no choice but to stop. So I do, and somebody immediately starts to swim over me, and somebody else kicks me in a more sensitive part. I feel the tightness of my wet suit as it clings to my chest, squeezing the air out of me like a huge black python from the deepest and darkest part of the Amazon. And still people keep swimming over me.

The first time this happened, I swam most of the 1,500 yards on my back. The reason for this is that once this basic primal fear sets in, it's all but impossible for me to stick my face under water. The mere act of turning on my belly and submerging my face fills me with the dread and illogical terror.

Over the years, and with much practice, I have trained myself to swim through this terror. Once I find my swimming groove, and my heart rate and breathing settles down, I can build to a descent swim. I have done this by starting out slowly, and by not kicking, to keep my heart rate low. But no matter what I do, I know that I will always come as close as possible to meeting my maker at the start of my next race. And that's why for me, the start of a triathlon is always the hardest start of them all.

The Joy of Swimming

There is a special moment when I first get in the water and push off the wall that I use to get myself into the pool. It feels like flying. I'm completely submerged, weightlessly gliding through the silky water. The only sound is that of the bubbles as they rush past my ears. The outside world is completely gone, and it's just me with my own thoughts and the gentle warm water as it slips past my skin. This moment is complete and full of promise. It lacks nothing and wants nothing. But all too soon it runs out, like my breath, when I burst above the water and take my first stroke.

I think of this moment on cold Colorado mornings when it would be so much easier to stay in bed and sleep for a few more precious minutes. The problem is, of course, a basic one. It takes so much more mental energy to get to the pool than it does to run or bike. To run or bike, all you really have to do is put on your gear and head out the door. That's it. Perhaps the refrigerator and the promise it holds might distract you, but if you can avoid the kitchen, you are well on your way.

But swimming is a completely different animal. You not only have to avoid the kitchen, but pack all your gear, make it to the pool, get changed, ignore the siren call of the hot tub, and jump into the cold water. As President Bush might put it, you've just spent a lot of your workout capital.

I swim with a local masters class a few times a week, and I find that unless I have a coach, I really don't have much workout capital left to motivate myself to swim. With a coach and a few lane buddies, I'm forced to push myself.

Do you know what L^2 (L squared) means? Long and Lovely… that's what my coach likes to see when we swim. (There is a swimmer's vocabulary that I had to learn when I first began swimming.) As always, I like to set the bar low. When I swim, I use a simple guide - "Try not to suck." I know that's not really positive motivation, but for us non-life-long-swimmers it will have to do, especially when you're next to a lane of master collegiate swimmers. Because these aquamen and women are fast, they have an effortless stroke that I admire as they glide through the water at tremendous speeds.

Now theoretically, I'm supposed to be able to able to swim at about ten different speeds ranging from easy to 10, 20 and all the way up to 100 percent effort. However, I find I only have three speeds.

1) Easy This is the speed I swim at 90 percent of the time. It consists of a stroke that somewhat resembles the ideal free-style form, but is about 90 percent slower than most of the swimmers in the pool. It does have one big advantage though. That being that I can breath. The other two speeds lack this essential swim technique and that's why I seldom use them.

2) Fast This is the speed I use when the coach tells us to swim 50-yards easy and 50-yards fast, or 50-yards build, or 50-yards negative split, or 50-yards at a strong effort, or 50 yards over kick, or 50 yards at 90 percent.

My fast speed actually consists of two speed settings. The first 25-yards or so is what you might actually consider fast. (Just for your information, about the speed of a motivated penguin waddle.) The second 25-yards consists of a lot of thrashing and flailing and heavy breathing with little forward progress, about the speed and direction of very drunk penguin.

3) Fasy Fasy is speed somewhere in between fast and easy. Properly defined, it is the speed that I swim after a fast swim. It is a rebuilding speed that gets me back to easy. It is not the thrashing and flailing and heavy breathing of a fast stroke, but it's also not yet the relaxed "I'm able to breath" speed of the easy stroke…but it's getting there. It's fasy.

What I find really fascinating about swimming is how different it looks from above the water than it feels like in the water. For instance, at my top speed I feel like I'm powering through the water like Superman soaring through the heavens. But if I were to look at myself from the above the water, I would look like I'm out for a leisurely Sunday morning swim.

One day I told this to a lane buddy of mine and he said that it was because water is 900 times denser than air. That seemed like a reasonable explanation until I was out running hard and I was passed by one of the local elite runners like I was out on a meandering stroll. It seems the real explanation is the obvious one, I swim like I run: Fasy.

Which reminds me of a workout I had one day. Sometimes I swim with this great German coach. And he's very German. For instance, he'll give you a set like this, "You vill schvim von hundred meters at 1:35.5 followed by von hundred meters at 134.8…NOT 134.9." Which is fine except that I'm sharing the lane with this guy who has all the swim toys. You know— the paddles, the pull buoy, the so-called "swim fins," the giant "uber goggles," and the "swim snorkel" that bends up between your eyes. All he's missing is a butt-mounted propeller.

I can't make the interval and the coach says I need to keep up with turbo butt. And there's no way that's going to happen unless I put on my diving fins, which, by the way, the rotund retired guys wear at a masters class that I sometimes attend in my mom's Florida retirement community. These boys have massive beer bellies and are the shape and general hairiness of a pregnant Kangaroo. The coach will instruct, "Let's warm-up with an easy 50." Before I think about pushing off the wall, the retirement boys are there and back like fat and well-tanned Michelin men under water torpedoes.

By the way, have you ever noticed that when you swim you tend to bargain with yourself like a used Turkish rug sales- man? You know what I mean—you have this internal conversation like, "Self, if you swim one more set then you can call it quits and go get lunch." or "Self, just swim until the top of the hour and then you can jump in the hot tub." Why is this? This does not happen on long run or bike rides. I think I figured out the reason though. On a run or a bike ride we tend to be com- mitted to finishing the distance since you need to get back home. In the pool you just need to swim another 25-yards. The solution to this conundrum is simple. We need pools that run at least 1,000-yards long. There would be no internal bargaining if you were outside in the cold and your choice was to swim back to the start of the pool or to get out and walk back. I bet you'd be putting in at least a 2,000-yard workout every time.

Bee Free

The Swim

The swim, or as I like to call it, the "if I can only," as in "if I can only muddle through the swim, the rest of the race will be cake."

For most of us Everyman Triathletes, swimming is usually our limiter. By limiter I mean the part of the triathlon that limits our performance. In other words, the part that we hate! And yes, I know that there are always a few triathletes who seem to have been born with gills and webbed feet. (By the way, gills and webbed feet absolutely slow you down on the run.)

When I started swimming two years ago, the best nautical terms to describe my swim would be barge-like or super-tankerish. Today I'm still more of a tugboat than a speedboat, but I'm working on it. Here's how:

My goal here is to improve your swim. I won't bore you with the best drills to improve your speed, or the newest swim techniques, or my advise on if you should get a sleeved or sleeveless wetsuit, or if the wetsuit should be black or blue and make you look like an orca or a quintanaroo (whatever that is) or an Ironman. I'll leave that up to the experts.

I will bore you, though, with one drill guaranteed to make you drink the entire contents of the lap pool. We did this one day in my master's swimming class. The coach called it the Egyptian drill. Start by swimming a normal freestyle stroke with the exception of bending one leg (choose your favorite) at the knee skyward (kind of like the dorsal fin of a shark) while swimming and kicking as hard as you can with the other leg.

This particular drill is guaranteed to make you sink like a rock while you flail around for your life like a very drunk sailor who never learned to swim. Why is it called the Egyptian drill? Could ancient Egyptians not swim? Is this what they looked like after they fell into the Nile only to meet the awaiting teeth of the nearest crocodile? I'll leave that up to the experts to answer.

Anyway, back to my main point; how to best improve your swim. The answer, unfortunately, is the same as how to lose weight: eat less and exercise more. With swimming the answer is even simpler and thus more diabolic: swim more. Period. With this in mind, I came up with a few simple motivational techniques to get me in the pool that I am happy to share with you.

1. The Siren Call of the Hot Tub: As I'm sure you know, there are no hot tubs in the sports of biking or running. I suppose you can bike or run by a hot tub, but the chance of you actually getting into the hot tub seem rather remote unless you happen to be extremely clumsy. However, there is usually a hot tub where the pool is. I often like to trick myself into going swimming. I'll say, "Self... let's go for a nice soak in the hot tub at the club." And before I know it, I'm out the door and on my way to the club. Then after a nice leisurely hot soak in the bubbling water I say to myself, "Self, why not go for a bit of a swim to cool down since you're already dressed for it?" The next thing I know, I'm in the pool and swimming.

2. No Sweat: There is no sweating in swimming, or if there is sweating, you're not aware of it. If you're like me, you probably get pretty tired of getting hot, sweaty, and stinky. Unlike biking or running, swimming offers a refreshing change of pace. After a nice swim you are actually cleaner than when you started. Plus all that chlorine acts as nature's own pimple cream that dries out your skin.

3. The Perfect Tan: There is nothing less attractive than the running tan. Except perhaps the biking tan. The running tan gives you a red neck, red forearms, and a red nose from where it pokes out from under your running hat. The biking tan gives you a red neck, red forearms, red nose, red v-shaped chest tan and red legs, but only from just above your socks to just below you biking shorts. Now that's a sexy look sure to make your honey swoon. On the other hand, the swimming tan *is* the perfect tan as long as you include enough backstrokes.

4. Bikinis and Speedos: There are no bikinis and Speedos in biking or running. This unusual lack of clothing by your fellow lane swim buddy can be a great motivational tool to get you in the pool. However beware as this can also serve as a potential de-motivational tool for some, especially if they describe their swim as being super-tankerish.

5. The Big Burrito: Please keep your minds out of the gutter here. Swimming makes me very hungry. Logically, I know that it does not burn as many calories as running, given the same amount of time, but swimming always leaves me starving. There is nothing more satisfying than a big burrito after a big swim. I like to say to myself, "Self...only 10 more laps and it's big burrito time." For you it may not be a big burrito, but it could be a nice mixed green salad or healthy soup. Beware. This could work as a super motivator for people like me. "Self...only ten more laps and it's mixed green salad time." I'd probably do an extra 20 laps with this motivation.

6. Bee Free: I've been stung four times in less than a year. However, never in the pool.

To recap: the best reasons to get in the pool and swim are very clean, perfectly tanned and cleared skinned hot guys and gals in Speedos and bikinis in hot tubs who don't sweat (at least not so you can tell) who enjoy the occasional big burrito and mixed green salad in a bee free environment. Now go out to the pool and give that Egyptian drill a try and let me know how you did.

4
Buying a Proper Bike
and Other Cycling Stories

Bear Beware:
In Search of the Perfect Tri Bike:
(Part 1)

So, I'm standing at the cash register the other day waiting to pay for my new bike when this short guy (wider than taller) gets off the same model bike I'm about to buy (in a smaller size) and says, "I'll take it." He spent a grand total of about 22 seconds test riding the bike. I, on the other hand, had spent three months of pain-staking work visiting every bike shop in Boulder and Denver, not to mention the countless hours on Google researching the perfect tri bike.

Let me take you back a few months to the beginning of this search for the Holy Grail of Triathlon: the perfect bike and the perfect bike fit. There is a kind of art to the perfect bike fit that is part science, part mysticism, and part blind luck. I just hope that the details of my quest will make your own quest that much easier.

I suppose my quest began at the Boulder Peak Triathlon when on a particularly fast stretch of road the left aero bar made a dash for freedom and flew off my old Trek 2100 bike (which I had somewhat clumsily converted to tri bike duty) like it was shot out of a cannon. Or perhaps it began a few weeks earlier when on a group ride my front derailleur would not shift out of low gear, leaving me sucking wind trying to spin, like the Road Runner runs, just to keep up. But I suppose it really began when I almost ran over that bear.

A few months prior, I saw my friend Luis and he said to me, "I'm going for a ride tomorrow morning in the mountains. Do you want to go?"

I said, "Sure if my run gets cancelled"...which it did...so at 5:00 a.m. I meet Luis and we're on our way. Did I mention that this was at 5:00 bloody *A.M.* You all know that means getting up at 4:30 a.m.

Luis says, "We'll have the roads to ourselves," and I'm thinking, *Sure, just us and all the drunks heading home after an all-nighter of boozing it up with their buddies.* Thank God for Bubba and Jeb. (Keep Reading.)

So anyway, once I'm awake and moving, I'm thinking, *This is not so bad.* Luis is pointing out various local birds flying overhead, and I notice that for the first time in my life there are no other bikes coming back into town. Even the prairie dogs are asleep.

We make a left turn, are in the canyon, and it is cold and still darkish. I get to mile nine up the canyon when my left leg checked out. I look down and the left cleat is turned sideways. I'm now officially hosed, as I don't have a wrench to fix it. Not a good way to bike unless you are in a Three Stooges movie. Luis is long gone. So, I turn around, head back down, and decide to go home the short way. The going is a bit doggy since I really can't clip in on the left side. I'm constantly looking down and trying to keep my foot on the backside of the clip.

About halfway up the last steep incline before the decent home, the sun hits. I'm feeling pretty good because I know that it's downhill in a few minutes. That's when I look up and see the biggest freakin' bear I have ever seen, and he's looking right at me. You take them out of the zoo, remove the bars and the pit, and boy are they big. Imagine a furry VW Beetle. At least that's what it looked like to me. I froze and almost pooped my pants. My heart jumped into my throat and my left foot flew out of the cleat. I stopped and looked at him. He was just kinda looking at me like a big hungry dog. His head cocked to one side, and I imagine him licking his lips.

Now what? I've heard bears can accelerate to something like forty miles an hour in five feet or less. Plus, I'm downhill from him. That makes it even easier if he chooses to go for an early morning triathlete breakfast. And there's no denying it...there's plenty of meat on my Clydesdale bones.

Have you seen those scary/crappy/rusty deliverance pick-up trucks that seem to ply the back roads of America? You know the kind of pick-up that's 40-years-old with booze buddies, Bubba and Jeb, in the front seat smoking just a little less than the truck. Well, thank God for Bubba and Jeb and their road burner. Just as the Bear was deciding which part of me would make the best breakfast burrito, one of these pick-ups comes chugging up the road. As the hill is very steep, the road burner was howling and popping and smoking and chugging and scrapping, which spooked the bear, who ran across the road and up a hill, which saved my butt, which went totally unnoticed by Bubba and Jeb, even though I stood there waving furiously at them to get them to slow down so I could use their truck as a bear shield.

Needless to say, I flew up the rest of the hill in record speed. Had Lance been in front of me he would have been bear chow. It was definitely then that I decided that I needed a new bike.

The O Bike:
In Search of the Perfect Tri Bike
(Part 2)

Nothing says you're a triathlete as much as a hardcore TT (time trial) bike. I remember my first triathlon. I rode a mountain bike with knobby tires and thought nothing of it. I began to have some serious bike envy as I got more into the sport. It always seemed to me that I was getting passed by athletes with better equipment. My first upgrade was to put thin tires on my mountain bike. Now racers on road bikes were passing me. I made the serious plunge and purchased a road bike. Now racers on road bikes with aero bars were passing me. I bought aero bars and put them on the road bike. Now racers on TT bikes were passing me and my bike didn't fit...at least not in the aero position. So I decided to take the biggest plunge and buy a TT bike.

I started my search at some of the local bike shops. Surprise! Nobody sells TT bikes. Sure they have glossy catalogue photos of the boys on the Tour with their teardrop helmets peddling space-age bikes to unbelievable average speeds. And yes, I can purchase the very same bike for a mere $5,000.00 with a few months wait. How about a test ride first? No can do unless you happen to be in the store four months ago when they had one TT bike for sale and it turned out that this bike was just purchased by a Peruvian triathlete visiting the States.

Lesson #1: Bike shops may sell TT bikes, but they don't stock them.

So, I kept looking and hoping, and my bike envy grew with each race over the summer. I noticed that all the best racers had one thing in common—their bikes ended with the letter "O"…you know like in Cervelo, Campagnolo, Sorrento, Bosso, and so on. So I began my search for the perfect O bike.

I decided that I had to have a Cervelo. I'd seen the boys on the Tour riding this fine machine, plus it had the coveted O. I went to my local Cervelo dealer, an upscale bike shop, and asked in a hopeful voice if I could test ride a bike. No go. This bike shop prided itself on building the perfect bike. The salesman was shocked that I would even consider buying an off-the-rack bike. "You see the factory supplied, ummm, how best to explain this?" he said, "low quality wheels (read crappy), and we cannot in good conscious sell you something with such shoddy wheels." He went on to explain that they only use the best: Zipp wheels. They'd be happy to use the Cervelo frame, but it had to have Zipp wheels.

"Ok" I said, "sounds reasonable to me. How much are the Zipp wheels?"

"Only $1,600," he said with a slight knowing grin. I did my best impression of a heart attack and staggered out the front door. $1,600 was my entire bike budget.

Lesson #2: Any level of TT bike will automatically cost $500 more and come with lesser components than the same bike in road form.

I went back to the computer and the Cervelo web site and found a dealer a mere hour from my house…without traffic. I called the dealer, and to my amazement, they had a very large selection of Cervelos in stock and ready to ride. That weekend I jumped on the highway and made my way to their shop. When I walked in I thought I had gone to Tri Heaven. They had something close to twenty TT bikes to choose from, including about eight Cervelos. I grabbed my credit card and headed to the counter. The tri department was manned by a little round man who was busy giving advice to a newbie gal renting a wetsuit for the upcoming Danskin triathlon.

"It should be very tight," he was telling this young lady as she turned purple. Her head was about to either explode or shoot out like a watermelon seed between the fingers of a nine-year-old.

I waited my turn. The next woman in line wasn't doing much better. Her ample breasts were not wetsuit friendly and the clerk seemed to be amused by her predicament. After a short lecture on why she needed a sleeveless wetsuit, he turned to me and asked, "What do you need?"

I explained that I needed help with the TT bikes. He said he'd call someone to come and help. I sheepishly asked if it was okay to take a bike for a spin, to which I took his non-reply as a yes. My bike envy was boiling, and I was so close to my perfect O bike that I could taste it. I picked the appropriate Cervelo (read: within my budget) and headed out the door for a test ride. I mounted the perfect O bike full of expectation of my very first ride. I was going to be the first and only one to ride this bike. WOW! I straddled the bike and stepped on the pedal. Nothing happened. I looked down. The bike had no pedals.

"Ahhhh," I yelled in desperation and took the bike back inside. The pudgy clerk was now huffing and puffing trying to wrestle the tight wetsuit from the first women. He had just managed to pull her, not the wetsuit, off the chair with a big thud. All the other sales people in the shop were very busy doing everything but helping customers. You know like stocking shelves, talking on the phone, filling out long mysterious forms, changing prices, and fixing the cash register. We, the customers, were all just standing around with our thumbs in our "you know whats." I had had enough. I pulled my thumb out and stormed out the door.

Lesson #3: There is nothing worse than not being able to have the perfect O bike.

Very Light, Very Comfy, and Very Cool: In Search of the Perfect Bike (Part #3)

I love my new bike because it is very light, very comfy, and very cool. Logically I know that it is a lot cheaper for me to lose six pounds than it is for my bike to lose six pounds, but we all know what a tiny role logic plays when it comes to weight loss. What's most amazing is that I can really feel the six-pound difference between my old bike and my new bike. I now soar up hills with or without bear motivation.

While looking for a new bike, I quickly discovered that there is a hierarchy, just as there is a component hierarchy, in bike frame materials. The list below represents available frame materials and is listed from the least to the most expensive:

Steel
Aluminum
Carbon Fiber
Titanium

The cost of these frames has a lot to do with their weight.

Steel bikes are strong, cheap, and heavy. I grew up riding a red, 10-speed, steel Schwinn Varsity. This bike took a pounding. In my neighborhood we had a bit of a 12-year-old bike posse that would cruise the neighborhood on blinged-out Schwinns. By bling I mean displaying big red flags on the back and baseball cards in the front wheels. We slammed the bikes over curbs, through homemade dirt mounds, and in and around back alley obstacle courses. When our folks called us home for dinner, we dropped the bikes and headed home, sometimes forgetting the bikes outside overnight. The Schwinn was very comfortable to ride as the steel frame soaked up the biggest bumps with conformable ease. The bike was tough and took a beating through the years.

My last bike was an Aluminum Trek 2100. Aluminum bikes are strong, a bit lighter than steel, and very stiff. It was also red and I bought it because it was on sale. However, I never really became friends with the bike like I did with my first Schwinn. The problem was that the bike was just too big and too long. I always felt like I was riding a massive bull, a very big and stiff aluminum bull, trying to cling to the horns as it bucked and bounced. The disadvantage of aluminum is that it is incredibly stiff and tends to beat up its rider on long rides. I suppose that also depends on your definition of a long ride. I simply define a long ride as any ride that gives you baboon butt. I tried to relieve baboon butt on the Trek by moving the seat way up. Then I bought a split seat. Then I bought a shorter stem. Then I bought the thickest biking shorts I could find with what Pearl Izumi assured me was the latest in Astronaut inspired materials technology. Why astronauts would suffer from baboon butt is still a mystery to me. None of this worked; it just made the bike twitchy and scary in corners. In the end I got used to it, but it never felt right. I really just wanted to feel comfortable.

It was this simple realization on the long ride home from the Cervela store that dawned on me like a ton of steel bricks…

Lesson # 4: Purchase a bike that fits well, is light and comfortable, and *not* because it ends with an "O."

I was going to be doing my first Ironman in three weeks, and I realized that I would not be breaking any speed or time records on the bike, so what was the real advantage of a race-ready tri bike? Not much if my goal is to simply finish strong.

This thought is incredibly freeing as it opened up the entire world of road bikes for me. I was no longer craving the perfect tri bike. I just wanted the perfect bike fit. It also meant that I could afford a better bike frame since I was no longer paying a premium for a tri bike. Carbon fiber was now on the menu.

Carbon fiber, one of the newest bike frame technologies, has the best advantages of steel (comfort) and aluminum (strength) without the downsides of heavy weight (steel) and inflexible stiffness (aluminum). Plus my new black bike is sleek with a really cool organic shape that is only possible with carbon fiber. It also has the added benefit of the new Ultegra 10 speed components. For the longest time I thought that the number of gears on a bike was just a pure marketing ploy by the manufacturer. In other words, the lowest and highest gears never really changed. Instead, Shimano only increased the number of gear choices or intervals between the gears. I thought, *do I really need thirty choices versus "just" 27?*

It turns out I was wrong. My new bike actually has a higher high gear and a lower low gear. This means I can go faster before I run out of gears and climb steeper in a smaller granny gear. Riding my new bike for the first time on a long ride (century) was an eye-popping realization like the old drunk joke:

A drunk was proudly showing off his new apartment to a couple of his friends late one night.

When they made it to the bedroom, they saw a big brass gong next to the bed.

"What's a big brass gong doing in your bedroom?" one of the

guests asked.

"It's not a gong. It's a talking clock," the drunk replied.

"A talking clock? Seriously?" asked his astonished friend.

"Yup," replied the drunk.

"How's it work?" the friend asked, squinting at it.

"Watch," the drunk replied. He picked up the mallet, gave it an ear-shattering pound, and stepped back. The three stood looking at one another for a moment.

Suddenly, someone on the other side of the wall screamed, "You idiot, it's three o'clock in the morning!"

It was kinda like that for me: you idiot, the new technology really is better!

Lesson #5: Buy the most technology you can afford since it is a lot harder for you to lose weight than for your bike to lose weight.

Stop, Stretch, and Smell the Roses

The other day I was on a "short" 40-mile bike ride with a friend when we hit the turn around point. Just before the short climb up Rabbit Mountain, I decided to stop on a small bridge and stretch to try to help the planters fasciitis in my right foot. I told my friend to keep going and that I would wait and meet him on the way back.

The sun was out and quickly chased away the chill of the morning. I took off my jacket and began to stretch. For the first time that day, I noticed the spectacular snow-capped Rockies. There was a gentle breeze caressing my cheeks. In the surrounding fields hardy mountain flowers were yawning and spreading their purple pedals. A small stream gently ran beneath my feet as a curious bluebird jumped from rock to rock searching for stray worms. I sat down, leaned back on the rallying of the bridge, closed my eyes, and felt the warmth of the sun as it played across my body.

It was just a few short minutes ago that I was working hard flying down the road thinking of nothing but my cadence. Trying to concentrate on keeping the same cadence up hill while spinning my feet downhill. In the back of my mind was that ever-present fear of cars and crashing. The front of my mind only concentrated on the cadence of the moment and keeping up with my friend. The world around me meant nothing more than the pavement flying past my wheels.

As I sat on the bridge perfectly still and happy, it reminded me that the sport of triathlon could be a jealous mistress. It can easily become all-consuming. As age-groupers we often strive to do longer races at faster times. One way to achieve this is to train like a pro.

In a nutshell, the issue is that many pros are young, single, childless and actually get paid to train and race. We, Everyman Athletes, tend to be older, married with families and actually pay to race. That means that in order for us to train like a pro we have to give up a lot...sometimes too much.

A friend of mine recently got divorced. He and his ex-wife started out the way most age-groupers do in the sport, by having a goal to finish a sprint triathlon, which they did. But they caught the bug. Next came an Olympic distance race, which took more training. Over the years the half-hour jog turned into the daily one-hour run. Their two kids began to see much less of their parents, especially the mom, for she had some natural talent and success.

In her middle thirties the wife decided that she had the potential to turn pro, or so she believed. She threw herself into the sport with reckless abandon. Perhaps it was for the love of the sport or perhaps it was to make up for something she was missing in her life. Like many women, she had spent much of her life caring for the family. It was now her time to spend on triathlon.

As in any divorce there are always two sides to the story and this one is no different, but triathlon was certainly a central character in this sad drama that ended up in a broken family. I suspect that triathlon has played a similar role many times, for triathlon is a most jealous mistress.

Have you ever been to an all triathlete party? I have and the conversations can be pretty dull. They tend to go something like this:

Triathlete 1: So how you doing today?
Triathlete 2: I'm pretty tired since I swam right after my recovery run.
Triathlete 1: How far did you run?
Triathlete 2: I ran an easy 5 miles today, but I ran 17 miles yesterday.
Triathlete 1: Yeah, I know what you mean, I just biked 70 miles, and I'm a bit tired as well.
Triathlete 2: Yup.
Triathlete 1: Yup. I think I'll go home and take a nap.

Not only is the conversation a bit dull, but only a triathlete considers recovering from a 17-mile run with another run. Many people would consider a 17-mile run a great accomplishment, but for a triathlete it's just another day of training.

Another problem with training hard is that you can't really get up at 4:00 in the morning, go for a swim, go to work, come home, cook dinner, do the homework with the kids, run on the treadmill, and do it all again the next day...at least I can't. To start with, anytime I run or ride over a certain threshold distance, I need a good nap to recover.

The pros I know nap all the time. In fact, they get paid to nap. They'll get up in the morning and go for 3,500-meter swim followed by an easy 6-mile run. They eat then take a long nap to give their body time to recover before they go for a longer afternoon run or ride. More importantly, they can do this because they not only get paid to do it, but they also have the support of their family. Triathlon is their fulltime day job. Most of us don't have this arrangement. We have to punch the clock and put bread on the table before we can train. But more importantly, since triathlon is not our day job, we don't have to train so hard. We don't have to sacrifice our lives in the name of a faster few minutes in our next race. Nobody is sponsoring us, so nobody is calling and wondering how come we didn't do so well, and yes, what about that money we are paying you to win?

So while triathlon may be a jealous mistress, we don't have to pick-up the phone every time she calls. We have the luxury of sleeping in on the weekends and of having a beer or two with our friends. We can use triathlon to complete our lives, not to rule our lives.

We can stop, stretch, and smell the roses.

Why I hate Spinning™

I hate spinning almost as much as I hate going to the dentist for a root canal. I would much rather take a long and pointy screwdriver and slowly stick it in my ear than take a spin class. This is somewhat ironic since I really love to bicycle.

Never let it be said that we here at Everyman headquarters only criticize. Indeed we are always striving to improve our sport by providing constructive ideas on how to correct and improve perceived problems. With this in mind, here's a short list of spinning issues and some simple solutions.

Issue 1: Lack of Any Forward Motion

What I really hate about spinning is that, unlike real bicycling, you don't go anywhere. You spend all this time and energy pushing the pedals and you don't move a single smidgen. You just sort of sit there like a very aerobic lump on a stump. This total lack of forward motion inevitably leads to a total lack of accomplishment. At least when you have finished a real bike ride you've seen a bit of the world and have put some miles under your belt so you feel like you've done something...not so after an hour of spinning.

Solution: The George Forman Spinning Chicken Rotisserie

How much wattage do you suppose 20 to 25 people spinning put out? I'd bet enough to power a decent sized chicken rotisserie. Imagine a small chicken rotisserie in the center of the spinning room (next to the coach). As the room starts spinning and generating power, the rotisserie comes to life with the warm amber glow of a cooking chicken. Now the room shares a common purpose and goal: to spin until the chicken is a delicious golden brown. If you slack a bit, that frozen chicken will never get done. Best of all when you've finished you have not only have a great sense of accomplishment but lunch as well.

Issue 2: Big Hairy Butts

When I'm on my bike outside, I look around and behold the full splendor of nature's creation as it unfolds before my eyes while I ride. When I'm spinning I behold Ralph's big hairy ass just a few feet in front of me.

Solution: The Spin Thong

Just like biking has its own fashion, it's time for spinning to get its own clothes. Since spinning takes place in the warm and comfortable shelter of your neighborhood heath club, we could certainly do away with the heavy black cycling shorts. My suggestion is the light and airy spin thong. Now you have something to look at. You'll just have to make sure that you get the "right" bike just behind the fittest athlete to behold the splendor of nature's creation. Word of warning…you don't want to be late to this class to avoid the getting the "wrong" bike and behold the splendor of Ralph's creation.

Issue 3: Standing Up

Most spin classes remind me of a Catholic Sunday mass. You know—sit, kneel, stand, pray. In spin class you basically get the aerobic version of same thing: sit, stand, sit, and spin. I don't know about you, but on a typical bike ride I stand about 5 percent of the time. For some unknown reason in spin class they make you stand about 95 percent of the time. And I hate to stand on a spin bike with a burning passion. Since unlike a real bike, the spin bike does not rock back and forth when I stand, causing my femur to pop-out of my hip with every painful rotation.

Solution: Limit Standing to Cruise Ships in a Hurricane

From now on standing and spinning will only be allowed on Cruise Ships sailing in seas of at least 20 feet or more. Because that's about the only time that your typical spin bike will lean the same 25 degrees that you normally rock it when you stand up while actually cycling.

Issue 4: Unsightly Sweating

I know that I sweat when I bike because I drink like a fish. However one can't tell by looking at me. The air rushing past my body does a pretty good job of drying the sweat long before it forms beads of moisture. Best of all, the harder I work, the faster I go, and the more the sweat evaporates. Of course this does not happen during a spin class. Indeed I'm sure that I could get a second workout just by swimming to the door from all the sweat pooling on the floor.

Solution: The Zip Lock Spin Bag

I'm sure you know that seventies fashions are hot right now. I seem to recall that sometime in the late seventies everybody wore these gray water proof workouts sweats that were meant to help you lose weight by keeping the body hermetically sealed in a sort of giant zip lock bag. Let's bring these back, and make them clear so that they don't hide the spin thong. Just zip yourself into one of these Spin Bags, and not only will the room stay dry and sweat free, but you'll be stylin' with that latest seventies trend. To complete the look, don't forget the knee-high socks with the red dual red bands.

Issue 5: Her/Frau Spin Kommandant

Like many people, I don't take well to being told what to do. And who yells at you more than the Spin Class Kommandant? "Sit down, now stand up, now give me three turns left and two turns right, now stand up again and speed up, now sit and slow down." Do you ever hear a please and thank you? I bet not.

The Solution: Mutiny on the Bounty

When the Spin Kommandant gets a little too big for his or her own britches, the solution is obvious. It's time for the people to rise up and take control of the means of production. And in my perfect idea of a spin class that means the George Forman chicken rotisserie. To be fair, you may want to give the spin instructor one warning like, "If we have to stand one more time, you'll pay the price, mate." And if they refuse to listen to reason, you may want to remind them that more than just a chicken can fry during this class.

Issue 6: Adjusting the Unadjustable

Today you can spend more money on a proper bike fit than on the bike. Yet the new spin bikes have dozens of adjustment possibilities from seat height and angle to handlebar height, length, and angle to finding the correct bike with the correct shoe clip. All this makes getting a proper spin bike fit about as likely as having a spin instructor that won't make you stand 95 percent of the time.

Solution: Hit the Road

Here's a crazy idea: how about dusting off that bike in your garage and hitting the road? I'll take the high road and you take the low road and I'll leave spin class far behind me. And my real bike and I will never part again because of the funny funny…you get the idea.

5
Running on Empty

Code 45

Sometimes the triathlon gods (small g) like to send subtle messages. You can listen and obey, or you can stubbornly keep going and pay the price.

So I awoke way early on the day of my first morning masters class. I was about 20 weeks out from my next IM and was starting to get a bit more serious about my training. I had almost forgotten how hard it is to jump out of a warm bed into a cold pool. In fact, I probably had forgotten because when I arrived at the health club, I arrived sans swim gear. Don't you hate it when you spend all that mental energy to just get your butt out of bed and to the pool, only to get there and not be able to swim? It's the worst of both worlds. Not only do you miss your workout, but you also miss that really great early morning sleep.

I was both tired and pissed-off at myself. I plopped down on the bench and thought about my options. I could go to the lost and found and "borrow" a swimsuit and goggles from the lost pile. This option appealed to me until I remembered there's a secret underground swimsuit Mafia at my health club. I can't prove this, but I believe that someone or some group has been trafficking used swimsuits at my club. There were too many times that I had forgotten my blue Speedo swimsuit in the locker room only to have it not end up in the lost and found. Low and behold a few weeks later there was some big guy in the next lane wearing a slightly used blue Speedo. Was it my Speedo? I had no way of proving it except to give him one of those long Larry David looks from Curb Your Enthusiasm. And since I'm usually not wearing my glasses when I swim, I could never really see the other guy's reaction.

Needless to say, the thought of some big guy giving one of these looks that morning as I'm wore a "borrowed" lost and found swimsuit filled me with dread. Besides it would sort of be like borrowing anonymous used underwear and that's just not my style…no matter how much chlorine is in the water.

Just as I was about to head home, I noticed that I have my running gear in my bag. I decided that since I couldn't swim, I might as well run, and I headed up to the treadmills. My luck had changed. I was just in time and on the right day for the morning treadmill speed workout. My club has a coached group treadmill speed workout that meets twice a week. The coach reserves a small number of treadmills and teaches the workout as a group.

My lucky day, I think to myself, as there was one treadmill open. Coach Mo said I'm welcome to join the group, so I jumped on the treadmill feeling all warm and fuzzy inside. Maybe I didn't waste my morning after all? This was true until about five minutes into the warm up when the treadmill shuddered, burped and stopped. The display read: "Code 45."

Code 45…what the hell was a Code 45? Was it some secret code that meant, "this dude is way to big and heavy for me" or "you know you must be pretty thick that you just don't listen."

Coach Mo gave the treadmill a stern look and hit the reset switch. It buzzed back to life with glowing red light glee. I pushed the start button and increased the speed. When I got past six mph the treadmill shuddered, burped and stopped. Again is read: "Code 45."

Coach Mo reset it and it died again just past six mph. Now you can't really do a very speedy speed workout below six mph, so you'd think that I'd get the message. But being a stubborn triathlete, I was hell bent on getting in a workout.

Coach Mo came to the rescue. He handed me a sheet of printed paper, which had the entire workout on it. You know, how far and fast to go and at what intervals. He suggested that I use the older treadmills on the third floor, which are almost always free, even during the busy morning hours. So I thanked him and headed upstairs. And sure enough there were two treadmills available. I picked the less sweaty one (or is it sweated upon one?), and dialed-up the speed to 8 mph...no problems... and I was soon sweating and running. About five minutes into the workout, I increased the speed to ten mph. At that point I was really running fast and hard...almost sprinting. My heart was pumping, my legs were working, and the ground was jumping.

However the triathlon gods were not happy. I had completely ignored their fair warnings and now I must pay the price. Without any warning what-so-ever, the treadmill came to a dead stop and completely died. I'm not talking about a slow and gentle deceleration. This was a dead stop—here and now. I came within an inch of hurling from the treadmill and executing a perfect triple salkow with a double twist off the front of the thing. Luckily I just sort of slammed into the display bar with a big thud that knocked the wind out of me. My speed workout was now officially done.

I suppose the moral of the lesson is that I ought to have listened to the triathlon gods. I need to take a Code 45 every-so-often. Perhaps we all need a Code 45 every-so-often. As triathletes we tend to be hard driven "A types" whose priority is to overcome adversiy no matter what the price or situation. It is in our nature to never take "no" as an answer. We will climb every mountain and forge every river. We will accomplish our mission or die trying. But sometimes I forget that I need to go backwards to move forward. My body needs rest to recover. I need to pay attention to subtle and not so subtle signs and just take a day off. More importantly take a guilt free day off. And that's what I figure is the real message of a Code 45.

A Code 45 means it is all right to not workout today and especially to not workout today and not feel guilty about it. Or to flip it around, a Code 45 means to take a well-deserved break and enjoy a no workout, a no guilt day with your favorite friend and favorite wine.

Or it could just mean, "This dude is way too big and heavy for me!" After all, the triathlon gods are pretty fickle.

My Secret Training Partner

I have a secret training partner. Her name is Happy, and she always makes me happy. But before you start thinking that you typed in the wrong URL—like www.happyending.com (and no, I have not checked if this is a real URL, but I'll bet it just might be) let me explain. Happy is a four-year-old Golden Retriever and we like to run together.

But that's not really what makes me happy, even though it makes her really happy. She can be a bit of a pain to run with. Today on our short run (four miles) she got into some mud and thistles, which I'm still trying to get out of her fur. She also likes to chase rabbits, birds (I don't think she's figured out the entire flying thing yet as she always seems to believe any bird is just one hop away from being caught) and her current favorite, sniffing others runners' or walkers' crotches.

All this combined with her complete fear of horses and cows and complete lack of fear of cars, bikes, trains and bigger mean dogs, always makes for challenging runs. Not to mention that she has recently taken to pooping right next to the trail, which means I'd probably win any race that included carrying a plastic sack of steaming dog poop for about four miles.

We got Happy as a puppy from a breeder who also breeds avalanche rescue dogs for the local ski patrol. Now avalanche rescue dogs have to love the outdoors, they have to be fit, and pretty smart, and most of all they have to love people. Happy is all of these things. However, what I forgot about avalanche rescue dogs is that first and foremost they have to love to dig. In fact a good avalanche rescue dog is bred to dig. And boy does Happy love to dig. My back yard currently resembles the surface of the moon if the moon's surface was a bit more Swiss cheese like with giant holes and craters. In fact, there is one hole that I have now filled up about fourteen times that she keeps excavating. To any Wal-Mart executive reading this, I believe that I am now very close to having a first rate railroad tunnel to China in my backyard for your entire Asian product needs.

No, the real reason that Happy makes me so very happy is much more subtle. Unlike anybody else I know, Happy never has any other place that she needs to be. She's completely happy and satisfied to be with me. She's never expecting or taking a phone call during our run. She's never rushing to another meeting or dinner. When we are together, her world is all about me.

And unlike anybody else I know, Happy never complains or makes any sort of fuss. I will get up at some crazy hour like 4:30 a.m. to go for an early morning run and she's waiting by the door ready to go with me as if I had just offered her a once-in-a-lifetime opportunity for fame and fortune. Never mind that it is freezing cold and dark outside. She's completely happy to head out into the dark and cold with me. And unlike anybody else I know, Happy will always come when I call. No matter how smelly or disgusting the unidentified chunk of road kill or dog urine she happens to be sniffing is, she always comes running to me when I call her name. I'll yell out her name, and she'll look up from the smelly treat, pin her ears back and come charging down the path to be next to me.

I grew up with a much different dog. My childhood pet was a tiny little apricot toy poodle named Tootsie, which my folks purchased for my grandma, but fell in love with and kept as the family pet. Don't fret though; we got granny a different white poodle named Suzy that ate like a goat. My grandma discovered that Suzy loved to drink coffee with her cake. Yes, the dog ate cake and drank coffee from her doggy bowl. This was not so much of a problem as was the fact that when she drank the coffee, she tended to get her long ears soaked in it. It wasn't too long before Suzy had unsightly coffee stained ears. To solve this problem, my grandma would tie Suzy's ears together above her head with a dew rag so that the dog looked and acted like a furry-wired gangbanger from the South side of Chicago.

But this problem was nothing compared to the issues that we had with Tootsie. Tootsie was not the sharpest puppy in the litter. She may have been the cutest, but she certainly wasn't the smartest. To begin with she had a perpetually itchy butt, which meant that she loved to drag her ass across the floor using only her front feet. When she did this, she got what looked like a huge satisfied smile across her face. She especially seemed to relish this interesting habit when my mom gave dinner parties for the neighbors. Now I was just a small kid so the sight of the dog dragging her butt across the carpet in a room full of neighbors didn't strike me as unusual, but my Mom was horrified while my dad stood dumbstruck by the scene.

This was really only a petty quirk compared to the time that my friend's dog, Midnight, (also a poodle) decided that the stuffed toy I had won at a local fair resembled something akin to the female of the canine species. I was a bit older and Steve and I had just returned from trying to impress one of my first dates with my prowess at throwing rings over bottles at a local fair. I had indeed succeeded in winning a giant stuffed panda, which I had left in the living room at Steve's house while we went with the girls to the kitchen to meet Steve's parents.

When we returned to the living room, Midnight (named so because he was black as night) had apparently succeeded in wooing the stuffed panda into giving up her, or perhaps his, virginity with his poodle charm. The dog was extremely busy going at it with the panda to the horror of both Steve's parents and my first date. As Steve is very Italian, I suspect the dog had plied the panda with his father's homemade wine before charming it with a doggy debonair gaze and substantial manly, or is it doggy, wit…which was now on full display for all to see. Midnight just smiled and seemed to suggest to my horri-fied young date that she could be next if she played her cards right. The panda just took it with a grin that seemed to say it needed a cigarette.

Tootsie never met Midnight. I suppose this was a good thing since Tootsie was no giant panda, plus she was fixed.

But Tootsie did have her share of other troubling habits. Number two on that list was her propensity to run away. Whenever I opened the front door she shot out like a lightening bolt on her way to Nebraska. Somehow the lack of food or shelter never bothered her. I can't begin to tell you how many hours I spent wondering my neighborhood yelling her name, and looking for her.

And that's why my secret training partner always makes me happy. Happy doesn't drag her butt across the carpet, she never drinks coffee, she always comes when I call, and I've never even so much as seen her even wink at a giant stuffed panda.

What to Do with All That Stuff?

If you're like me and you've been training and racing for a couple of years, you might find that you've accumulated a lot of stuff. Everything from old race numbers to finisher medals to old running shoes. Which, of course, begs the question: what to do with all that stuff? Here are a few interesting ideas and suggestions:

Old Race Numbers

I remember reading somewhere that you should save your old race numbers, frame them in a decorative collage, and put them on the wall to have as a reminder of your glorious race days. I have a different idea. Most race numbers seem to be made of that special paper that does not tear (unless you pin it to your shirt at which point it tears immediately).

That's why I like to take my old race numbers and sew them into a quilt of shame. At night I use my quilt of shame as a reminder of all those races that I barely finished. As I snuggle under my quilt, I fondly remember my past races...*oh look there's the marathon where my legs locked-up at mile 20. I had to waddle to the finish line for 6.2 miles. And look there's the Ironman race number where I flatted eight times. Oh here's the half marathon that was so hot that I got tunnel vision, almost passed-out, and had to have my first IV.* What a wonderful way to fall asleep.

Finisher Medals

Over the years I have accumulated a pretty large collection of finisher medals. If you thought that they would be sized according to the distance of the race, you'd be wrong. My largest medal is from a local 5k Turkey Trot I ran a few years ago in a tiny town next to my wife's hometown in the middle of Illinois. It seems that the more obscure the race, the bigger the medal. Keep this in mind next time you set your sights on the Boston Marathon. Perhaps you should be training for the annual Ogleby Turkey Trot.

I've always thought that all my medals would make for a great wind chime. But recently I've had a much better idea: to start you'll need about 10 dogs of different sizes and breeds. The medals make for great K-9 bling. There is nothing more stylin' than a hound sporting a gold and silver half marathon medal.

You'll of course need different breeds and sizes as the medals come in different colors and sizes. For instance, you would not want to put that huge Ogleby Turkey Trot medal on a tiny toy poodle. That would look just silly. The best part of this idea is that the more races you run, the more dogs you can make over with their own doggy bling.

Running Shoes

If you're like me, you probably have a closet full of old running shoes. They say that you are supposed to replace your shoes every 300 to 400 miles of running, a number that keeps dropping. I'm sure Nike is working on disposable running shoes as I write this.

You could donate your old shoes to charity. There are a number of great people and agencies that collect old running shoes and ship them to places in Africa where folks really have no shoes.

However, I have another idea. We all know that running shoes are made of super cushioning sole material. Why not put this technology to use where it's really needed…your car's bumper. Over the years the automakers have refined the traditional car bumper to the point that if you happen to lean on a modern bumper too aggressively, you'll either scratch or dent it.

I have great solution—just take those old running shoes and glue them (sole out) to the most likely impact points on your bumper. Now you have a car that's not only ready for the local mall, and any potential fender bender, but more importantly says to everyone, "This driver is a serious runner!" (That is, of course, when he or she is not driving to the local mall to buy new running shoes.)

Cotton Race T-Shirts

With the advent of new technology like "Coolmax" breathable fibers, many of us now have drawers full of old cotton race T-shirts. If you're lucky, you may have a brother-in-law or sister-in-law who would love these old school workout clothes. Why? Because you know that nothing says, "I'm a hardcore weight lifter like a well-worn and properly torn cotton t-shirt."

If you are not lucky with the family connection, here's another idea. Seal-a-meal those shirts and place them in storage. Why? Because you know that 20 years from now nothing will say that you're a hardcore old school runner like an old cotton T-shirt. Sure…they may make your nipples bleed on any run longer than 5k, but that's just another sign that you're indeed a serious runner.

Water Bottles

Water bottles are certainly everyone's favorite race bag swag. They come in two varieties. The soft kind you can squeeze (good) and the rock hard kind that cannot squeeze (bad). Have you ever tried drinking from one of the rock hard kind that takes two hands to squeeze while running on a treadmill? Word to the wise, don't or you could find out how fast eight miles an hour really is when you catapult off the back of the treadmill into the glass partition wall of the nearby crowded women only aerobics class, who all stop and stare at you as you lay half-naked, splattered with your butt tightly pressed against the glass wall. (Not that something like that has ever happened to me.)

So, what to do with all those old water bottles? Here's a simple idea: they make great cat hats. Unscrew the cap, drill two small holes in it, tie a string through both ends, and put it on your cat's head. *Magnifique les chic pussy cat.* Now your cat will be stylin' with the latest cool cat cap. After all, you don't want to make the cat feel left out since your dog is wearing all that medal doggy bling. Do you?

Post Script: No animals were hurt in the making of this story.

6

Race Reports

Accidental Personal Best:
The Harvest Moon Triathlon

The sun had just risen and I was coughing and feeling pretty cruddy as I walked my bike to transition. I really had no business racing, let alone racing a half Ironman, and I knew it. My coach had told me to bail, my mom had warned me that I would only make myself sicker, and my gut told me they were both correct. So what the hell was I doing in transition getting ready to race?

The week had begun poorly. My young son's nasty cough was diagnosed as walking pneumonia. Tuesday he was put on some antibiotics and I was beginning to cough. Thursday he was back at school, and I was at home. Friday I got my dose of antibiotics when my cough turned nasty. So why on Sunday Morning was I standing in the pre-dawn cold shivering and racking my bike? A simple series of dumb decisions had brought me here. I had committed to giving a friend a ride, and being stubborn I had decided that, if I felt better, I would give the race a try. Why? Because I had paid $130 to race and there were no refunds.

One hour before the start of the race I made the smart decision and told my friend I was bailing. She understood and said that she could get a ride back home from another friend. We looked for her friend in the transition area for over 45 minutes. Fifteen minutes before the start of the race I made the dumb decision to race.

We found the friend, who, as it turned out, couldn't give my friend a ride home. Now my choice was to race or hang out for the next seven hours and watch others race while I waited for my friend to finish. Not racing was bad enough, but standing by watching others race would have been unbearable.

Five minutes before the race I made my last and best decision. I decided to use the race as just another training day, have fun, and drop out after the bike, or earlier, if I felt bad. I started the swim very slowly, embarrassingly slow. I normally jump in the water and swim like I'm the unknown chicken**** brother of the crocodile hunter being chased by a saltwater crocodile. I flail my arms. I kick my feet, churning up a magnificent rooster tail. About two and a half minutes into the race, I hyperventilate and desperately search for the rescue boats. The boats are of course impossible to find since you can't see anything at the start. So I stop swimming freestyle, switch to breaststroke, and muddle along for a few minutes until I get my heart rate down. At this point I repeat the entire process all over again. If I'm lucky, by the middle of the race I'm back to permanent freestyle and finally swimming with confidence.

This morning, however, there was no breaststroke needed. I just swam very slowly until I felt comfortable with my breathing. Instead of racing, I thought about lengthening my stroke, rotating my hips, and brushing my thumb against my thigh to complete the entire stroke. This was just another master class, so my time was irrelevant except...thirty-one minutes after the start of the race I was out of the water. I looked at my watch in disbelief. This could not be correct. I had just swum the fastest 1.2 miles of my life!

No matter, I was still not racing, just training and it was time to bike. I clipped in and headed out on the ride. I had decided to take a page from my friend Michael's winning book and go for a real easy spin. No standing up to power-up hills. No big ring for flying down hills. By the way, what's up with all the indoor spinning instructors that make you stand for about 65 percent of any spin class? I've never seen any pros riding over half a race standing up. And why don't those spin bikes free-wheel? After standing up for 25 minutes without a break, I always forget about this fun fact. Then the second I sit down, relax, and stop spinning, the damn machine almost pulls my femur out of the socket.

My new bike does freewheel and I took advantage of this. I coasted down the hills. On the uphills, I kept the bike in the small gears and the revs high. I spun and spun and spun and spun. I also made sure to slow way down at the aid stations and load up on tons of water and sports drink. Since I was not racing, why blow through the aid stations without refueling to save a few precious seconds? I also gave up trying to stay with all those guys with 42 on their calves.

The weather was beautiful, the road was smooth, the police had stopped all the traffic, and I was just going for a ride in the country except…two hours and fifty minutes later I was back in transition. This was 20 minutes faster than my last bike half-Iron distance bike segment. I thought that maybe the bike's computer was somehow broken. It had stopped working twice during the ride. This time could not be possible.

The half marathon was an out-and-back course. Just an easy 10k jog, I thought. I can do that and drop out at the halfway point of the run. I put on my running shoes. My legs were a bit sore, but nothing drastic. This was going to be just another easy jog like I did every Thursday morning with my running buddy. I was going to run embarrassingly slow, but so what, I was not racing. This also meant that I could walk all the aid stations and enjoy some unhealthy snacks like Oreo's and Coke every mile.

By the turn around point I was feeling tired, very tired. I also realized that dropping out would mean walking back the same distance as running back, so I turned around and ran. But since I was not racing, I walked the uphills and ran the downhills. I also began to really listen and to hear what the real racers were saying. It was amazing, they were saying things like, "Good work!" and "Keep on going!" and "You're almost there!" and deep down I knew they meant it. Didn't they know that I was not racing?

I looked closely into their eyes and saw the raw determination to finish. I saw all types of people from fat to fit. From young to old and they all had one thing in common, no...*we* all had one thing in common, and that was to finish. And even though I wasn't racing, I knew that I was part of something bigger; I had to finish. We all had to finish.

At mile ten, my calves locked-up. "Just a few more miles," said a guy with a 56 on his calve as he ran by me. "Keep on running!" And so I did.

I could now see and hear the people at the finish line and I realized that at this point racing or not racing was irrelevant. Just finishing with all the rest was what really mattered and so I did except...when I crossed the finish line the official clock said 5:50. That was just under an hour faster than my best half Iron distance race: a new accidental personal best. Not too shabby for not racing.

The Worst Triathlon Ever

I knew the white doves were a bad omen. A very bad omen indeed. Watching them circle Boulder Reservoir in the early morning sun, my stomach tightened, and my skin crawled. Why they decided to release about two-dozen doves at the start of this year's Boulder Peak Triathlon was a mystery. Perhaps the race organizers wanted something different and special to mark the new ownership of the race? Perhaps God wanted to show his hand? Perhaps I was over analyzing this and just feeling my typical pre-race nerves?

It was a wave start, and as usual I was in one of the last waves. They put the older competitors in the first wave. I guess to give them a head start and keep them from racing during of the hottest part of the day. They put us buff Clydesdales at the end. I suppose they figure we'd drink all the beer if we finished first.

We waited around for about 25 minutes as the different colored caps hit the water. At last it was our turn. I knew my wife and buddy were a few waves ahead. The water was warm, too warm for a wetsuit and too late now to worry about it. The starter was one of the first racers to complete the Hawaii Ironman. Just as he was about to blow the horn for our wave a speedboat came flying by with an obviously rattled kid screaming, "Stop the race! A guy died!"

Very suddenly everybody grew quiet. You could hear the waves lapping at the shore until the sirens broke the early morning calm. About 500 yards ahead was a rescue boat with a wetsuit-clad body and several first responders performing CPR.

We stood quietly transfixed in the early morning sun as the boat rushed to shore and to an awaiting ambulance. No one had signed up for this. "There's no dying in Triathlon," I almost said out loud. This was a day for celebration. A day for achieving and surpassing personal goals. A day for putting all the training to a test. A day to enjoy.

Could that be my wife or friend in the rescue boat? I immediately thought. My stomach sank lower. No way to know. So we all just stood there watching and worrying. The start of our wave was delayed until the ambulance drove away.

I was still worried and a bit shaken-up as I started up Old Stage Road on my bike. Old Stage Road is the signature hill and feature of the Boulder Peak Triathlon. It may not have a viscous name like the "Beast" in the St. Croix race, but it is never-the-less just as steep and daunting. The reward for climbing Old Stage is a very fast descent on the back portion. For big guys like me, it is not uncommon to reach speeds of 50 mph.

As I crested the top, I was ready for the descent. This is where I can usually make up much of my time. Not today! About halfway down the hill the volunteers were yelling at us to stop. A racer had crashed just ahead only minutes earlier. He had slid down the hill, crossed over the centerline, and slammed into, and remained trapped under, a Honda that had been heading up the hill. The firefighters were trying to extricate him from beneath the car. He was alive but in obviously critical condition as signified by the whirling blades of the flight for life helicopter coming in for a landing.

This was turning into a triathlon like no other I had ever experienced. I breathed a small sigh of relief as I went up the hill that marks the start of the run. *What could go wrong on the run*, I thought? It took about five seconds to get an answer.

A guy running toward me on the return portion of the run looked drunk. He was weaving back and forth, stumbling over his feet, and wheezing. I was about to ask him if he was okay when, with a dull thud, he face-planted on the blistering hot concrete next to me. I stopped and yelled for help, which came immediately since we were very close to transition. I continued my race a bit unsteady on my feet as they worked on the fallen runner. I seriously began to wonder why I was racing. Triathlon seemed such a hollow, selfish, empty, and pointless pursuit in the big picture. I asked myself, "Why am I doing this? What's the point?"

I was finally able to answer those questions when it occurred to me that triathlon, especially the Iron distance, is a lot like life. Both start with a struggle in water. A violent watery beginning where the only sound is that of your own breathing. Like childhood and the teenage years, the swim is self-centered. You know others are around but you don't and can't really acknowledge them. Full of energy, you struggle and race as fast as possible to the next phase.

Like the middle years, the bike is the longest and easiest part. It becomes much more fun and social as you start to interact with others around you. A sense of shared adventure is born. It is also the part that can make or break you. Still full of strength and confidence, you push ahead as fast as possible to the next phase.

Like the golden years, the run is the culmination of all your hard work. By now, you most likely know how well you'll do. The run is the most social with a real sense of shared struggle and purpose. While some are still competing, most now encourage each other, measuring each step against a personal and internal goal. Some now looking ahead to the finish, as the run is also the hardest and most painful part. But many don't want the finish to come. They realized that they have worked long and hard to make it this far.

And perhaps like death, the finish is the ultimate reward. You can finally stop running; your work is done. You've come full circle back to your loved ones. They are at the finish waiting for you with hugs, kisses, and an easy ride home.

Post Script:

The runner who fell spent one week in the hospital with renal failure from dehydration.

The biker who crashed under the car was extricated after about 40 minutes and flown to the hospital with numerous serous injuries. He survived but remains partially paralyzed.

The 76-year-old swimmer died after remaining in the water for over 20 minutes before being rescued. He was an avid swimmer, runner, and cyclist who started entering triathlons regularly at the age of 70. His death was ruled to be from natural causes. The Peak was his 6th triathlon of the year. I suspect he died on his own terms: doing something he loved. His last race took him on an altogether different course that followed the white doves. And I am almost certain that many of his friends and family were waiting for him at that final finish line with hugs, kisses, and an easy ride home.

Racin' Wilma:
Surviving My First Hurricane
and Iron Distance Race

The sweat dripping down my forehead, over my nose, and onto my lips had the rank taste of defeat. If I were the crying type, I would have been balling my eyes out. My stomach felt sick, the kind of sick you feel when the phone rings in the middle of the night because you know nobody ever calls with good news in the middle of the night.

I was over six miles into the bike portion of my first Iron distance race and had just flatted for the third time. Worse still, I had already used both of my spares. I couldn't believe I was finished. It was a small miracle that I was even in Orlando. Just a few days ago, Hurricane Wilma had been forecasted to ravage this part of the state. The strongest Hurricane ever measured was still heading straight for us, but she had dallied over Mexico for a few days longer than expected. I suppose she liked Cancun. I don't suppose Cancun liked her.

To make matter worse, I had a great swim, just over 1 hour and 12 minutes for the 2.4 miles, and was feeling really strong. I spent the last 12 months getting ready for this one day. Getting up at 5:00 a.m. to take long cold bike rides with the bears. Countless early morning laps in the pool, not to mention the endless runs and a long bout of planter fasciitis. And now, the latest nerve jarring game of hide and seek with Wilma.

This really sucks! I thought as I sat in the hot and muggy field feeling sorry for myself as one racer after another passed me by. Except not all of them passed by. To my complete surprise one guy stopped and asked me if I needed anything. "Sure," I said with a bit of sarcasm, "how 'bout an inner tube and a CO2 cartridge?"

"No problem," he said and handed me both. I was too shocked to thank him, so dude, wherever you are, "Thanks!"

I hold a great appreciation to the Great Floridian Triathletes (2005) who helped me on the bike course. I didn't know it yet, but that was only the beginning of a very long day. Before the end of the bike portion, I would flat five more times. Four flats on the front wheel and four flats in the back wheel. I would sit in five other fields waiting and begging for help. This gave me ample time to think about why I race and how I got here.

Setting the bar really low, that was my new triathlon strategy. Without knowing it, that had also been the strategy that I'd used over the past five years to get to this point and distance in my triathlon life.

Here's the strategy in a nutshell: when you set a goal make it really easy and doable. In other words, your goal should be something very simple like: I want to finish a sprint triathlon this year. That way when you meet your goal you'll have the hunger and determination and willingness to surpass the goal next time. If you set the bar really high, like: I want to finish an Iron distance race in under 12 hours; chances are you'll blow up, miss the goal, and become discouraged with yourself and the sport.

It really comes down to why many of us do this crazy sport, I thought as I got back on my bike after fixing the flat. We do it to challenge ourselves and prove that we can finish something that most folks would never even contemplate starting.

But, back on the bike after three flats, I knew that there was something seriously wrong with my back wheel. I started to suspect a problem with the spokes poking through the rim tape on the inside of the wheel that might have been puncturing the inner tube. You just don't flat three times in seven miles on the same wheel.

I rode on slowly with the bitter taste of defeat still fresh in my mouth. I had no spare tires, no spare air, and 50 miles to go before getting back to the transition area for my special needs bag which contained two additional spares and air. Every time the road surface changed, I suspected a fresh flat. I was being passed by the middle of the pack. My expectations had gone from finishing in 13 hours to just finishing.

I suppose that an Iron distance race is 30 percent physical (if you've done the training), 30 percent race-day nutrition, 30 percent mental and 10 percent luck. My luck had run out at mile six. My mental condition was unstable at best, and that meant that my nutrition plan was quickly falling apart. I rode on too terrified to lean the wrong way, too terrified to speed down the hills, too terrified to hit the brakes hard and too terrified to flat.

Somehow I made it around the first loop. I was ecstatic again. The roller coaster of emotions had just crested the top. I was going to finish the race. My special needs bag had two spares and two CO_2 canisters, and besides I had made it 50 miles without a flat. "The wheel must have sorted itself out," I said to my wife, who had caught up to me at end of the first loop. She offered me her spare tubes, but I declined. I was all set to finish I thought as the emotional roller coaster sped down hill. A mile later my front tire went flat. By now I had become pretty fast at changing tires. After less than five minutes I was back on the road thinking that I had had a real flat.

A mile later the back tire blew flat again (number four on the back wheel) and my world collapsed with it. The emotional roller coaster came flying off the tracks and crashed and burned.

It's funny how high you can get in a race and how fast you can slam into the ground. Mentally I had just belly-flopped onto hot pavement. I knew there was no chance what-so-ever that I'd finish the race now. I only had one last spare. It was at this point that I mentally reset the bar to zero.

It's like that with expectations. The second you lower the bar, that's the moment you can truly race. Have you ever noticed that some athletes who were really good at say swimming when they were young have a hard time with the sport as they enter the "masters" years of their lives? They'll never meet, and certainly never exceed, the best swim meet times from their youth. Their expectations have been forever set beyond their waning abilities, and thus they are always swimming up-hill, unlike us non-swimmers where every new milestone is a triumph.

I had no expectations anymore, and thus nothing really mattered anymore. My time didn't matter, the blazing heat and humidity didn't matter, and the other racers who kept passing me didn't matter. There was simply nothing I could do but change the tire and see how far I could go before the inevitable next flat. This stark realization is completely freeing and completely wonderful. To my surprise it brought with it a powerful sense of purpose and clarity. I knew what I had to do and what I needed; I needed duck tape and I had to fix the wheel.

I accomplished both when I flatted right in front of a water station for the run part of the race and asked around for help. Fortunately, two of the volunteers actually had duct tape in their cars. Best of all, the cars were parked directly across the street. I tore the tape and created my own rim tape, put in on the back wheel and fixed the flat. I couldn't fix the front wheel, as I had no air to re-inflate the tire. But I was sure the back wheel would now hold for the rest of the second loop. Little did I suspect that the front wheel would decide it missed all the attention I had lavished on the back and would flat another thee times.

We were parked some 90 miles into the bike ride at the last water stop before the Buck Hills (three large rolling hills that challenged both body and spirit just before the very steep Sugarloaf ascent). *Clermont must be the only God forsaken place in Florida with Colorado sized foothills*, I thought as my thighs seized-up like vise grips. And the Great Floridian must be one of the only Iron distance triathlons that puts the biggest hills last.

Eight flats had sent me from the tip of the spear to the butt of the spear. We were a rather motley bunch consisting of big girls on mountain bikes, the long-ago retired and yet still very driven, the old school types with shin length red-stripped socks, the unlucky, the unprepared, the unwise, and two guys on vintage bikes with strap-on-pedals instead of clips. These boys were drafting off each other like Lance and Hincapie, however at the butt of the spear where no one monitors or cares about it.

We all had that deer caught in the headlights look as we sat in the shade at one of the last the water stops and contemplated the up-coming hills and bike cut-off time. Except that there was no water. The race organizers somehow had assumed that because it was 90 degrees with 90% humidity, we would be drinking our own sweat. All they had left for us were warm lime Gatorades. Have you tried to chase a warm Gu with straight warm Gatorade about nine hours into a very hot race? It is sort of like gulping green battery acid.

We did have one last advantage. The heat, humidity, lack of water, and common goal had forged a deep bond between us. It was this bond that had saved my sore ass. Long ago I had run out of both inter-tubes and air. It was through the kindness of this motley band of racers that I was able to even contemplate finishing the bike. Except that I didn't care anymore. I had fixed my last flat and I knew it. You see, in my dazed state of mind I forgot to repack my tools. I left them in field number eight somewhere about 20 miles back and that was that. I was sick of fixing flats, and I was sick of the bike. All I wanted was to be done with this ride from hell.

It's funny how fast you go from training all year, to wanting to really compete, to just wanting to finish. Now a new thought crept into to my mind - I had to finish *because* of the eight flats. I had worked too hard and survived too much not to finish. It was this thought that propelled me up the Buck Hills and up Sugarloaf. It was this idea that got me back to the transition area, this thought, and a hell of a lot of luck. *May the air stay in your tires, and may the wind be at your back and not in your butt* had be my new race motto.

I finished the bike in just under nine hours and squeezed in under the bike cut-off time.

Don't ever run a marathon before your first Iron distance triathlon. Why? Because if you do, you'll know exactly how far and how difficult the 26.2 miles will be on you. It is indeed a very strange and daunting feeling starting a marathon at 6:00 p.m. at night after a 112-mile bike ride. The mind says you must be crazy and legs whole-heartedly agree.

The sun was going down and I was mentally fried. It seemed that in a distant life I once lived, I had imaged myself crossing the finishing line before sunset. Now I was hoping to come in before midnight. I quickly gave up the notion of hammering the marathon. The difference between a 16-hour race and 15-hour race was pretty meaningless. Besides, my legs would seize-up like a stray cat at a dog shelter every time I broke into the slowest of jogs. I just wanted to finish and perhaps start to enjoy the race a bit.

I met my wife on the first part of the run, which was an out and back 10k before three loops around Lake Minneola. She was running back and I was sort of walking (if you consider Frankenstein's gait a walk). She looked great with two sponges tucked into her shirt. This was when she earned the nickname Sponge Barb. We stopped and chatted. She told me that she had lost her Blackberry cell phone on the ride when she hit a big bump. I tried to express my concern as I was pounding on my thighs to keep them from locking-up. We had decided to bring our cell phones so that we could encourage each other during the race. She was really depressed; but more importantly, she was way ahead and really doing great.

I, on the other hand, was at the wrong end of my marathon. During the first 13 miles, I ran looking like my best impression of Frankenstein growling and terrifying the local villagers. In my case it was the other competitors and aid station helpers. I seemed to have done a proper job because by my second loop many of the aid station helpers had cleared out.

Somehow, by mile fourteen I was feeling good. I was (to my never-ending surprise) the only one running at this point and perhaps the only one on the course. Hurricane Wilma had scared away many of the racers so there were only several hundred in the race to begin with, and most of them had finished already.

There was only a small handful of us left running in complete darkness into on-coming traffic (the state law in Florida) on a road with no shoulder. Every so often I'd spot the bouncing glow of a green light stick ahead in the pitch-dark Florida night. I'd run up to them and we'd start chatting. It was nice to have company, especially on the far side of the lake loop, which was now pitch black and very spooky in the gathering gloom of hurricane Wilma.

I caught up to a friend I had made the night before at the pre-race dinner. We almost hugged in the starless night and started chatting. He told me that he had found the strangest thing on the bike ride: an almost new Blackberry. And yes, it did turn out to be my wife's Blackberry.

Barb was there waiting for me when I crossed the finish line just before midnight. My beautiful Sponge Barb was there with about 30 other folks who stuck it out in the starless night. It was nothing like the Ironman finish you might view on television. Nobody said, "You are an Ironman," except for my wife who had done terrifically well by overcoming her fear of the swim. She swam a blazing fast 2.4 miles and set the fastest Mica family record for an Iron distance race.

And while technically I was not an Ironman, I was a finisher. I was hoping to check this goal off my list and move on to others. But now, with so many flats, I'd have to race again just to see what time I could really finish in. Besides, I'd set the bar so low that I couldn't help but surpass my goal the next time. Ironman here I come.

May the air stay in your tires, and may the wind be at your back and not in your butt.

Post Note:

I took the Shimano wheels to the bike shop where I had purchased my new Giant and had a long and serious chat with the manager and boys in the repair department. They examined the wheels and pronounced the plastic rim strip that lines the inside of the wheels to be cheap, misarranged, and most likely the cause of my trouble. They replaced it, at no charge, with a higher quality Italian brand. We'll see.

The Road to Kona

The Road to Kona is a hilly one. When you watch the Kona Ironman race on television the bike course seems flat. But when you actually get on the road to Kona you are immediately surprised by how hilly it is and by all the crazy graffiti. More on that in a second.

I arrived in Kona, Hawaii last week for just one day of fun in the sun. By the way, "AlooooHA," (as they say in Hawaeee) to all.

I arrived by cruise ship tender right next to where the swim starts. I went to Kona to frolic in the surf and sun with my family, but was immediately amazed at the number of triathletes swimming the course. There's a tiny beach, about the size of your average garage door, tucked into the corner of the bay. You can climb down a few small steps to reach the "beach," pass by kids snorkeling, and you're on the swim course.

The beach is outlined by a series of buoys that mark the course and distance, and you're free to swim 2.4 miles by following the buoy line straight out into the bay. The warmth, clarity, and saltiness of the water immediately took me by surprise. For those of us who normally swim in a pool, it takes a bit of getting used to. Trust me, you don't want to open your mouth, as I did during the first few strokes.

The salt water settles in the back of your throat, making you immediately thirsty. This is not a happy feeling for the 2.4 miles of the swim. What creates a happy feeling is the scenery. There are numerous colorful small and surprisingly big fish swimming below the surface. So many in fact that I had a hard time concentrating on my swim stroke. I'd take a stroke and immediately notice some big-ass fish a few feet below me. *Oh look at the size of that fish*, I'd think to myself, then: *Holy crap is that a shark?* There were definitely not sharks in my Colorado pool. *That can't be a shark; it has an orange stripe, Phew!* A few strokes further down the course and I'd spot another big-ass fish. *Is that a shark?* I wondered as I tried to judge the dorsal fin for its sharkiness factor...and so it went while I swam.

A pleasant surprise was the warmth and buoyancy of the salt-water, which made swimming feel like I was in a wetsuit. I Every so often I would stop, terrified that the fish below me was indeed a man-eating shark, only to notice how easily I floated without kicking...which was good as I thought kicking might attract sharks! Just for the record, as far as I know no-body has ever been even remotely eyes-up, let alone attacked, by a shark during the race. But these fears are not logical, so I did a lot of floating and wide-eyed staring down.

A quick word about the waves—they are pretty big for the most part but also mostly harmless. I've come to accept that big ocean swells are actually much easier to swim in than small choppy lake waves. The ocean swells pick you up and gently put you back down. The small choppy lake waves break over your head, which makes it hard to breathe and see. I'll take the Kona swells, thank you very much.

Now I wish I could report that I actually rode a bike on the course, but remember that I was in Kona to frolic in the surf with my family. So I did the next best thing. I drove to a beach that happened to be on the bike course. This means that I drove about 25 miles of the bike route. I can report back that it is surprisingly hilly. I believe that it officially has about 6,000 feet of elevation gain. This is pretty considerable when you consider that the big island is also very windy.

I always believed that the Hawaiian trade winds were soft and gentle. Sort of like God giving you a gentle puff as you sit on the pristine beach under the gently swaying palm trees. After all, this is what the postcards like to show. Forget it! The wind comes howling across the Pacific at something like 15-25 mph. It hammers you in the face and threatens to blow off any loose articles of clothing like hats or poorly tied bikinis.

I rented a Tony Soprano-sized Chrysler 300 and even that was blown around as I drove the course. *Toto were back in tornado Kansas,* was my main thought as I wondered how hard it would be to peddle 112 miles into this wind.

At least you have the Kona graffiti to look at and to keep your mind occupied as you hammer into the wind on the bike course. The course is lined with hundreds of messages written in white rocks. The volcanic ground is mostly jet-black and the locals have taken to spelling out messages with white rocks across the jet-black ground. Many of the messages profess a deep love for this guy or that gal. But there is a fair share of triathlon graffiti that encourages racers along the course.

I'm not making this up. My wife spotted a message that said, "Go Roman …2005!" Roman, whoever you are, I hope you did our name proud and kicked some serious butt in last year's race!

By the afternoon it was time for us to head back to our cruise ship, and I was stunned at how warm it had gotten. The black lava radiates heat and the hot winds don't do much to cool down the place. We drove by the Natural Energy Lab. This is where the running course makes a left and heads into the lava field for a four-mile loop toward the sea before heading back to town. I felt hot just thinking about it while driving in the air-conditioned splendor of my rented luxury cruiser. I was also stuck in stop-and-go traffic. I have to admit that my dream of island paradise does not include traffic. But here I was stuck like a bug in a rug. Creeping slowly forward, I looked down at the speedometer and figured at an average speed of six mph, it would probably take us longer to get back to town than the pros take to run the course. Of course the difference being that I was sittin' back with the air blowing in my face, jamming to island music, while they would be running 26.2 miles in blistering heat with hot winds through a jet-black lava field. All of a sudden the big-ass fish didn't seem so bad any more.

Here's an idea for the WTC. Any chance of making the swim last in Kona…just a suggestion. Mahola!

$\underline{7}$
Great Tips and Some Wise, or is it Wise Guy, Words

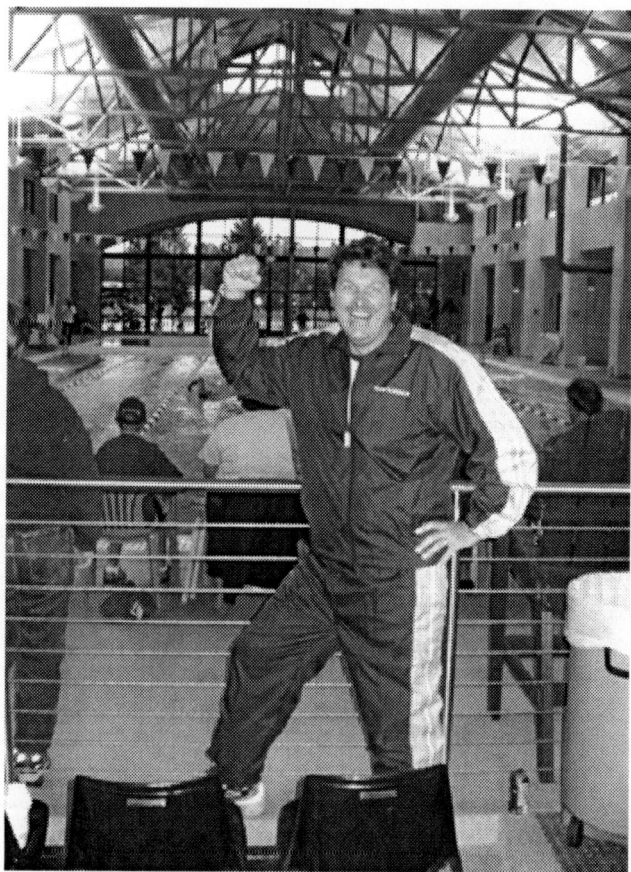

My Top Ten Secrets to a Personal Best Time

Over the years I've learned a thing or two about achieving a personal best race time. If you're a newbie to triathlon, I think these secrets will serve you well. Here are my Top Ten Secrets to a Personal Best (PB):

10) Find a Comfortable Race Outfit and Wear it for the Entire Race

I recall one of my first Olympic distance races. I flew out of the pool (this was a pool swim), headed outside toward transition only to be stopped dead in my tracks by a bare butt sighting. Now there is nothing wrong with a bare butt at the right time and the right place, and this one happened to belong to a rather curvaceous triathlete. However this was neither the right time, nor the right place, for anything else...including changing into bike shorts.

Transitions are free time, so don't waste them putting on your favorite biking shorts and jerseys. I've raced in my Descente triathlon gear for up to a half Iron distance race. Descente does a great job designing racing clothes that you can wear swimming, biking, and running. You too can race like the pros by investing in race gear. Transitions also tend to be a time of profound confusion for most of us. Why add another layer of worry by changing clothes?

Once a year I race this little local sprint triathlon that I use as a baseline measure of my fitness. Last year I improved my time by about ten minutes, five of which came from a faster transition time. While I understand that five minutes may not seem like a lot, but try lowering your 5k time by five minutes.

I'd bet that'll cost a lot more time, effort, and money than a new race outfit.

9) Aero Bars

I started my triathlon career on a mountain bike. Over the years I kept upgrading my bike until last year when I spent what I considered to be a big chunk of change on a new carbon ride. But the biggest difference in my bike times came when I started using aero bars. This could be because aero bars put you in a more aerodynamic position. But I suspect that it has more to do with feeling like a real triathlete. Almost nothing says triathlete more than aero bars (okay, shaving your legs as a guy also screams triathlete... among a number of other non-tri-things). I really believe that the more you look and feel like a pro triathlete, the more you'll race like one.

8) Get a Coach or a Training Plan

You don't have to have a desire to compete in Kona to need a coach or a plan. There is so much from a technical point of view to the sport of triathlon. It is much more than just the sum of three sports. For instance, you may be the best cyclist on your biking team, but when's the last time your raced a 27-mile time trial after swimming and before running? Or when was the last time you just raced a 27-mile time trial? Most bike racers stay in a pack and draft off one another. They don't race alone until the end of the race. This is a world away from what you need to prepare for a triathlon.

How about you newbies out there, what's your training plan? I'm sure most of you have done some running, but how do you combine it with swimming and cycling? How do you combine training for all three sports in such a way that you actually grow stronger and fitter while not injuring yourself? Simply put, you need a coach or a plan.

7) Put Your Swim Goggle Strap Under Your Swim Cap

This is a quirky tip, but when you race I recommend that you put the goggle strap under your cap like the pros. That way if somebody happens to hit you in the face and knock your goggles off, they'll stay around your head. And yes, people may kick you in the face in an open water swim.

6) Figure Out Your Nutritional Plan

The longer the race, the more important your nutrition becomes. This is a simple two-part strategy: 1) Figure out what works best for you, and 2) Train like you race. And always remember to bring your own food. There's a good chance that the race may not have your preferred gel or drink, which can result in a complete disaster.

During the summer of 2005 I raced a half marathon. I always have a peanut butter and jelly sandwich before a race. Not this time. I didn't have peanut butter, so I switched to cereal. The swishing mixture of milk and Gatorade as I ran proved to be an explosive combo at about mile seven. I still feel bad for whomever had to clean out that porta-potty.

I stole my best secret race supplement from my 8-year-old son. I love to eat Smucker's Uncrustables during my race. They come individually prepackaged so they don't make a mess. I like to freeze them the night before so that they are ready to eat on the bike. Best of all, they are about 300 calories each. For me this is the perfect amount of fuel for a strong run time.

5) PEDs Performance Enhancing Drugs

Some pros may have access to such banned substances as Erythropoietin (EPO), steroids, and even the ultra expensive Human Growth Hormone (HGH). However, the rest of us also have access to our own Performance Enhancing Drugs (PED). They are called Advil, Tylenol, and Motrin. Anyone can pick their favorite pill, but I definitely use one of these over-the-counter painkillers before, during, and after a race.

My personal favorite is Advil as it does a great job in numbing some of the pain from a lifetime of sports injuries. As an added benefit, most of these legal drugs also help reduce swelling and inflammation after a long race. And this is a very good thing, as those of you who have completed a long race of any sort will surely know.

Legal Disclaimer:

Everyman Triathlon has little to no medical training beyond stopping a bloody nose or removing a hangnail. We advise you to consult your physician before using any medication.

4) Visualize Victory

The week before your next race, take about 15 minutes each night and situate yourself into a quiet place with no distraction. Try to remove all the daily clutter from your mind and visualize the race. By this I mean see yourself in the water swimming with a strong and steady stroke. Visualize yourself running out of the water and putting on your helmet, your biking shoes, sunglasses, and heading out onto the bike course. Did you notice what I just did? I completely forgot to see myself removing my wetsuit. That's why you do this every night before the race, so that at race time you know exactly what you will do, and how you'll do it.

By the way, it is a lot easier to go back to transition for your gel in your mind than it is to do it in a race. More importantly, the other reason you want to visualize the race is to see yourself winning, or getting a PB, or finishing strong. You pick what you want to do, but the first step in reaching your goal is to visualize yourself doing it.

3) Get Yourself a Great Triathlon Mantra

A triathlon mantra is a verbal formula repeated in racing or training in such a way as to innovate a desired outcome. Now that's an eyeful to read, so here's the easy Everyman definition: It is a saying that you repeat in your mind that helps you overcome difficult moments.

My mantra is a simple one: "Fast, Smooth, and in the Groove" I know it may sound silly in the written form, but I use this one because it helps me stay focused on the basics:

1) **Fast** I want to make sure that I know I'm racing for a reason and that reason is to be as fast as possible. Some of you might not care about being fast and may want to use a different key word.

2) **Smooth** This word helps me keep in mind that I don't want to overdo it. I need to be fast, but at the same time I don't

want to bonk or push myself beyond my limits.

3) **Groove** This keyword is to help me remember all of the training that I did, and I utilize it especially to keep my focus on my form. To me "groove" means to maintain that long swim stroke, that powerful bike pedal rotation, and that perfect proud running form.

More importantly, I use the mantra when my thoughts turn negative. You know - when the pain, the heat, and the distance all conspire and threaten to make you crack. At that moment I say out loud, **"STOP"** and switch my mind to, "Fast, Smooth, and in the Groove." Give it a try. I bet it will work for you as well.

2) Write Down Your Goals

If your goal this year is to break a three-hour Olympic distance time, write down 2:59 on a bunch of post-its and stick them everywhere. Put the Post-it on your refrigerator so that you see the goal when you are going for that unneeded snack. Stick it on your rearview mirror of your car so that it gives you a reason to get to the club for that post work swim. Place it on your computer so that after you are done e-mailing friends, you'll remember to head out the door for that cold-day run.

There was a famous study which concluded that people who actually wrote down their goals were four times more likely to achieve them. So pick a goal and remember to make it measurable and attainable. Don't forget to stick it on your spouses or boy/girlfriend's forehead (or any place that you are likely to see often) so that you'll never forget why you are doing this crazy sport.

Now, what you have all been waiting for, the Number 1 Secret to a PB.

1) Lose Weight

It is so much easier to go fast when you are a lean and mean racing machine. Additionally, it is much more difficult to do this than it is to recommend it. For that reason I'll only give you one bit of advice. To lose weight you have to want something more than the food in front of you. You may want to fit into that race suit for your next race, or you may want to shave a few minutes from your run time. Think of whatever it is you want before you have that next cookie, and remember that it is always a conscious decision to eat more or to eat less. You have the power to slim down; it's just a matter of wanting it more.

Finally, here's another bonus secret. The real key to a personal best is to stay healthy. That means you can't forget the four basics rules of training:

1) Stretch before, during, and after training.

2) Don't overdo it. If it really hurts, don't train through the pain. See a Doctor!

3) Remember to warm up and cool down.

4) Get plenty of rest. In order to get stronger, your body needs time to recover.

The Ten Commandments of Triathlon

1) Resist the urge to discuss your workouts

You've done the work, so be proud *and* quiet. While a century ride may be interesting, telling others about it is certainly not...especially if they're not triathletes. Let your race times tell the story. There is nothing more fun than breaking a personal best and letting others wonder how you did it.

2) Eat healthy fuel

Meat, fruits, and vegetables. Sometimes there is nothing more satisfying than a huge meal of fried carbohydrates or processed sugar after a hard work out. (Read: soda and fries or cookies and cream) But you'll just put on all that weight that you've worked so hard to remove. What's the point of that? Keep in mind that the ideal body of a peak triathlete is that of a 1930's depression era farmer and you won't achieve that with super-sized calories.

Nutrition Tip: Brush your teeth after dinner. It will make you less likely to have that late night snack as you'll want to keep your mouth clean and fresh and the food won't taste good with toothpaste!

3) Go For It - for someone else

Pick a cause or a charity or a person and train and race for them. It will make getting up for that 5:00 a.m. morning workout much easier and more gratifying.

4) Race your strength, but train your weakness

If you are a great runner, spend more time in the pool. If you come from a swimming background, get to know the track. If you have a passion for biking, invest in some good running shoes and a swim coach.

5) Read a good book in bed

Don't forget to take some time to do nothing. Your body and mind will appreciate the rest and recovery time, and you'll have something (besides triathlon) to talk about at your next party.

6) Remember to thank your Ironsherpas

They could be your spouse, your siblings, your kids, your friends, or perhaps your parents. All those great people in your life that let you pursue this crazy sport by covering for you when you're out training, schlepping your stuff, and by being there for you at the start and finish lines.

7) Have fun too

Unless you have a sponsorship contract with a Tri Dudai or Nike, the results of your next race won't keep your kids out of college. Enjoy the race day and give that passing pro a hand because their paycheck really depends on how they finish.

8) Set measurable and attainable goals

"I want to race an Olympic distance tri in 2007," is an *attainable* goal, but it is not a *measurable* goal. "I want to finish an Olympic distance tri in 2007," is a bit better, but still not the ticket. "I want to finish the Chicago Triathlon in under three hours in 2007," is a *measurable and attainable* goal.

Notice the difference? Now that you have your goal set, paste it on your computer screen and your bathroom mirror so that you'll have a motivating reason to train.

9) There is no such thing as a "Sprint Triathlon"

Triathlon is an endurance sport. A true sprint triathlon would look something like this: 1) A 50-meter freestyle swim 2) One lap around a Velodrome 3) A 100-meter dash. For this reason, to succeed you must be the turtle and not the rabbit.

10) You can't DNF in life

In life everybody finishes—some just finish sooner than others do. So while you're here, always remember that triathlon is a great way to be alive!

New Year Etiquette Rant

The other day while my back was turned and I was asking the sales clerk a question, a small round man absconded with my shopping cart. He just grabbed it and scurried away like a fat, hungry weasel with a juicy chicken. So for all the fat, hungry weasels in the world, here's my New Years etiquette rant.

Swimming

There is no passing in lap swimming: When you share a lane you really have only two choices: 1) Split the lane, or 2) Share the lane. When you share the lane don't pass, because until they invent underwater rearview mirrors, the other swimmer will have no idea that you're attempting to pass.

There is no mid-lane parking in swimming: If you're halfway down the lane, you should only be doing one of two things - swimming or recovering from a cramp. Save the, "my cat barfed-up the biggest hairball last night" discussions for the hot tub.

There is no underwater treasure in the pool: Swimmers know that you can find some of the strangest stuff at the bottom of the pool. From old gum to funky hairballs to water soaked Band-Aids to what we all hope are dead bugs and small creatures of all sorts to much funkier stuff. Don't point this out to others. They've likely seen the dead furry thing out of the corner of their eye, and they're also trying to keep their lips closed as tightly as possible.

There is no lane splitting in swimming: When you share a lane, stick to your side of that lane. If you find it hard to stay on one side, I have two words for you: "Open" and "Water."

There is no road rage in the pool: Accidents will happen. If by chance when your lane mate is doing the fly and you're doing the breaststroke, and the two of you pass in a tight lane and they happen to slap you in the ass, and you happen to kick them in the crotch, just keep going. Perhaps you'll mutter a few words of apology, but these things happen in lane swimming. They probably really didn't mean to grab your ass and you probably didn't mean to kick them in the crotch. You both should know this and not use it to start a fight or a long-term romance.

If you have long hair, wear a swim cap: This goes for both gals and guys. Have you ever had a four-foot long slimy hair wrap itself around your neck, through your mouth and up your nose while swimming? I have and I can promise you that you won't make your interval or even finish your lap when you're caught in the tentacles of the human hair squid.

Cycling

No farmers wipe when drafting: Okay, I know that it is almost impossible to properly blow your nose when you are biking. And at the same time, the nose does tend to really run on those cold bike rides. But if you are part of a draft line don't even think about blowing your nose over your shoulder.

You better be able to ride like Lance if you dress like him: If you are wearing the matching Discovery Channel or T-Mobile shorts and jersey with a $300 aero helmet and are riding a $5,000 carbon fiber Madone, you'd better be fast. Words to the wise: there's nothing that stands out more on a bike then a rich guy with skinny legs.

If you don't know how to draft, then don't draft: Drafting and bike handling are skills that take time and effort to learn. Don't just jump on my back wheel on a whim because I happen to be a big guy and I easily break the wind (or perhaps just break wind). You never know….do you? Why? Because if you get it wrong we will both pay the price. If you want to draft, just ask.

Help other cyclists by the side of the road: We are a small band of fellow riders compared with the big world of cars and trucks. If you can help fix a flat or supply a spare air canister to a fellow cyclist you'll earn some big karma points. Because you know that one-day that'll be you sitting on the side of the road.

Ride single file: For some reason people driving cars are seemingly hell bent on killing cyclists. Don't give them a reason to hate us even more. Share the road.

Fat, Hungry Weasel Drivers: The next time a car feels the need to pass while leaving me with about two millimeters to spare, I hope they get an extended visit from tiny, horny, and extremely itchy anus worms. I hope these hell bent anus itchers set-up a homestead in their rectum and breed and multiply like bunnies on a sunny and grassy knoll in springtime.

Running

There is passing on the track: Keep to the outside lane on track when you are running slow or walking. For all you drivers out there, this may seem like a strange and foreign concept (I know you like to drive in the left lane at 55 mph with your turn signal on), but on the track let the faster runners pass on the inside lane.

Dogs like to sniff in the funniest places: If you have a dog, please keep it under control. While I love dogs, I would prefer to take it out to dinner and movie or two before we really get to know each other that well.

Dogs like to sniff in the funniest places: If you don't have a dog please don't get too mad. While I try to keep my dog under control, sometimes it will jump the gun and go for what humans might consider an inappropriate sniff. I truly apologize and I hope you understand that this is not something I encourage or do without a dinner and movie or two.

Just say "Hi": I like to acknowledge my fellow runners with a "Hey" or a "Hi" when I'm out on the trails. After all, running is such a solitary sport most of the time. So unless you are really seriously training to win the Boston marathon, just say, "Hi" back. I understand that you're serious about your running, but you can say "Hi" back because I doubt you'll win the Boston Marathon at a ten minute pace. And if you are a bit out of shape, you won't have a heart attack by uttering the word "Hi' back to me.

The Fountain of Youth

One morning I was standing on line at my favorite bagel shop when I overheard the following conversation between two avid elderly runners.

man: "So what did the doctor say?"

women: "She said that I need to stop running for a few months to let my feet recover."

man: "I know that's going to be hard for you to do."

women: "The doctor suggested that I take up swimming. She's a triathlete and that's what she does."

man: "How old is your doctor?"

women: "I think she's in her thirties"

man: "No wonder, wait until she's 79 like you."

At this point I jumped into the conversation and said, "I think swimming is great exercise, best of all it doesn't beat up your body like running does. You should consider it as a alternative to running."

Both of them looked at me like I had just suggested that they take a stroll to the moon. It's a look I've seen before. It says you must be crazy, do you know how old I am and wait until you are my age, and how could some young wiper snapper makes such a crazy comment?

I suppose taking up swimming at the age of 79 is pretty tough. On the other hand, I swim with an 80-year-old woman who started seriously swimming only a couple years ago. But isn't that really the other definition of getting old? Not the definition that is measured by years, but the one that is measured by attitude. Don't we all get more conservative as we get older? I looked up conservative in the dictionary and here's the definition: "Favoring traditional views and values; tending to oppose change. Moderate and cautious."

I think that we all get conservative as we get older, and I'm not talking about the political definition but the personal and emotional one. It becomes much more difficult for us to change our views and try new things. We have a lifetime full of experience, social expectations, and emotional scabs that prevent us from taking the plunge into something new.

For instance, my young son took up boogie boarding while we were in Hawaii. We went to the beach, he saw the waves and other kids playing in the surf, and he threw himself into the ocean. A few hours later he was riding the waves like an old hand. But for me it was harder. I knew what those big waves could do if I got it wrong. I didn't want to look silly out there, and I certainly didn't want to embarrass myself in front of my family and the locals. I had a lifetime of experience and fear to overcome, which I did. And I'm happy to report that the first big wave picked me up, slapped me around like an angry pimp, pulled off my swim trunks, and spat me out, butt naked, on the shore in front of my family and half the population of the Big Island. But I rode the next one…after I quickly pulled up my shorts and washed the sand out of my butt.

My friend, Fred, likes to say, "Time wounds all heals." And yes, I'm still a bit traumatized from being so forcibly stripped searched in front of the entire beach. But I figure my family has seen me naked and hopefully the locals thought I was some misguided German tourist. I think that's why I like competing in triathlons so much. It is difficult to be personally conservative and be a triathlete. The sport has a way of pulling you out of your comfort zone. For example, it's not too much of a stretch to be a collegiate swimmer or runner and compete in a masters level race. You spent your entire childhood on the track or in the pool, so what's so hard about racing when you turn thirty-something?

But with triathlon you don't have the luxury to just run and swim. You also have to bike. And since the sport is still new, there are very few, if any, thirty-something triathletes who competed in all three sports when they were young. That means that by definition most age-group triathletes picked up the sport, or a least parts of the sport, later in life. And to me that means that we are not personally conservative. Or if you want to flip the coin over and look at the other side, it means we have found the fountain of youth.

Funny thing, this search for the fountain of youth. People have been looking for it as long as people have been around. And for just as long other people have been making a living selling youth to those seeking it. The pharmaceutical companies have us believing that youth can be bottled and put into a little blue pill that makes your wee ready to whoopee. The doctors have us believing that youth can be restored with a scalpel, and nip here and a tuck there, and a few ounces of silicone placed in the proper locations. The diet purveyors would like us to believe that we can find youth by eating only meat or vegetables or fruits that begin with the letter z; or by avoiding all carbs on the first, third and seventh leap year; eating only happy fish, or it is sad broccoli? The cosmetic industry would like us to believe that we can apply youth to our skin through an ounce of a potion made from the bones of the Humuhumunukunuku fish that are combined in a sterile lab with seaweed and peanut butter.

The travel gurus want you to know that youth and happiness can be found in the glossy brochures of their packaged holidays to the sun trenched islands of the Bahamas, or the warm Caribbean waters of the Gulf of Mexico. The mall operators want you to know that youth can be found in the music filled stores and shops in the open and safe shopping arcade. The ancient Orientals would like you to believe that you can restore your youth and vigor by snacking on a diet of tiger penis, shark fins, and rhino horns. The tobacco industry wants you to know that youth can be found in the wispy cool and refreshing smoke of a menthol cigarette. But we know that that's all a bunch of Madison Avenue magic.

I believe youth can't be leased, bartered, or bought. It's free for the taking as long as you are willing to take it. And that's why I really love triathletes and the sport of triathlon. We're a small community of athletes who have taken up the challenge to stay young in both body and mind. We have shared attitude that life is for living. Given the choice of watching the tiger pass by or taking it by the tail, we choose the tail. And in this struggle, I believe we end up somewhere quite unexpected. We end up at the fountain of youth (and no, it's not in Florida)

Okay, so sometimes we end up butt-naked on the beach with sand up our ass, but I figure that's a small price for the fountain of youth.

Behind Every Great Ironman is an Ironsherpa

Do you get goose bumps watching the finish of an Ironman? You know that terrific late night drama of the finishing line as the Everyman competitors funnel in running, walking, stumbling, or even crawling across the line to the cheers of the crowd. It is one of the best moments of any triathlon, no matter what the distance, when you can actually witness the human overcoming all obstacles in vivid Technicolor. But what really gives me goose bumps is the wild crowd of cheering well-wishers. Because I know that this crowd is filled with the heroic stories of the Ironsherpa that made the finishers' race possible.

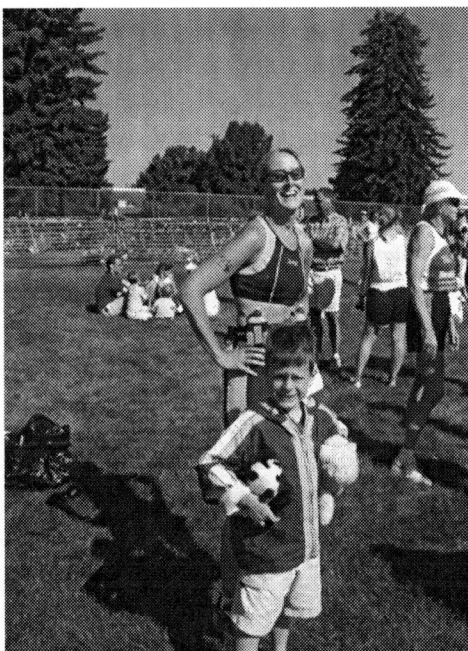

Who is your Ironsherpa? All triathletes have one. An Ironsherpa is the person in your life who carries your load so that you can train and race. It can be your husband or wife. It can be your mother or father, sister or brother, or perhaps your best friend. An Ironsherpa is that person in your life who puts up with all of your triathlon talk, who rubs your sore muscles, who cooks your recovery meals, who makes your bed on those early mornings, who takes the kids to school so you can swim, who understands why you prefer a long run to a good movie, who does not mind your constant dress code of workout clothes, who goes to the bike store with you and smiles politely while you discuss the merits of this or that wheel, who gives up his or her vacation plans around your race schedule, who washes your smelly socks, who buys your protein powder, who puts up with your bike lust, who works while you play, who makes your pre-race peanut butter and jelly sandwich, who took up running because you run, who understands why you're too tired, who understands why you really truly need to ride today, and who stands in the crowd cheering you on as you cross the finish line. An Ironsherpa is that person in your life who really deserves all the glory but instead gets most of the toil.

The 2005 Great Floridian Triathlon (GFT) was held just about a dozen hours before Hurricane Wilma slammed into the southwest side of Florida. It was during this Iron distance race that I came face-to-face with the incredible virtues that really make Ironsherpas so wonderful. It was a small miracle that the race was even put on. But the looming hurricane and last minute planning didn't make for a smooth race. Many of the volunteers who work the aid stations either didn't show up or left early.

Probably the best known feature of the GFT is a substantial climb on the bike course called "Sugarloaf Hill." Sugarloaf is no picnic to climb, and worse yet it comes toward the end of both bike loops. The summit of Sugarloaf is a popular place for Ironsherpa to watch and cheer on their friends and families. It's also one of the most anticipated, if not the most anticipated, aid stations on the entire 140.6-mile course.

During the 2005 GFT a small group of Ironsherpa showed up at the summit of Sugarloaf a little after the start of the race. To their surprise, the aid station was set-up but nobody was there to work it. The aid station crew never showed-up and thus the station sat partially stocked, but almost completely abandoned. Being true Ironsherpas, these fine folks rolled-up their sleeves and worked the aid station for the entire nine plus hours of the bike portion of the race. What's more incredible, when the aid station ran out of water, some of the Ironsherpa drove to a nearby quickie-mart and purchased a couple of cases of water, and kept handing them out to those of us still on the course. These words can't really express how grateful I was to have water at the top of Sugarloaf. Especially after many of the prior aid stations were long abandoned and completely dry.

I have my own special personal story of Ironsherpa gratitude. That's one reason why I'm just as happy being an Ironsherpa as an Ironman. During my first half Iron distance race I had a "bit" (quote unquote) of a problem on the run. It was extremely hot (90 plus) by the time I got to the run course. To make matters worse, there was not a tree or a bit of shade to be found. I had consumed enough on the bike, or so I thought, that I didn't need that bottle of now warm Gatorade I had left behind at the transition area. In fact I felt fine, so when I started on the run I decided to forgo the first two aid stations. By the third aid station at mile three I was getting a bit thirsty so I drank two heaping cups of water. The problem was that these cups were those little Dixie cups that we used in grade school. Two cups equaled about four ounces of water.

I kept up this "hydration plan" for the next several miles on the scorching run course. By about mile eight I was walking, and by mile ten I was getting tunnel vision. I was extremely dehydrated and didn't know it. But my Ironsherpa knew it.

With her help, encouragement, and guidance, I got the immediate medical attention I needed.

Now I realize that I was so far out of it that I was in no way thinking or acting rationally. I was very sick and ready to pass out, but I just wanted to keep going. It took only about 20 minutes in the ambulance before the IV fluids kicked in, and I was back to normal. Funny thing is that I still wanted to go back out on the course and finish the last three miles of the race. It took a while for me to realize just how close I had come to doing some real damage to my body. So feeling dejected, foolish, and completely stupid for having been such an idiot to let myself get so dehydrated that I dropped out of my first half Iron distance race, I sulked home to my wonderful Ironsherpa.

Instead of reminding me of how stupid and dangerous my lack of hydration had been, she took me out for an entire family victory celebration ice cream Sundae. As we sat in the local Dairy Queen eating the coldest and best Sundae of my life, she turned my train wreck of a race into a huge family accomplishment. She made the very best lemonade out of my sour basket of lemons.

So that's why when I watch the finish line of any triathlon I get goose bumps. For I know that behind every great Ironman is a greater Ironsherpa.

Why Do You Tri?

When you really think about it, life is a suicide mission. In the end nobody survives. You can't get away from this fact no matter how far you swim, how far you bike, or how far you run. So why do you swim, bike and run? Why do you tri? Have you ever sat down and thought about why you like this sport so much? What is it about triathlon that makes you so passionate in the embrace of this jealous mistress? Here are a few reasons why I believe that she completely owns so many hearts.

On Demand Lives

Modern life has become simpler, easier, and more convenient. There are very few basic necessities that most of us can't have at any given time of day or night. Are you bored? Just rent a movie or watch it on demand anytime of day or night. Are you hungry? Well Taco Bell is now open 24/7 as are 4,000 other restaurants. Are you cold or hot? Turn up or down the thermostat and go back to your taco while watching the latest Hollywood blockbuster. But in case you are becoming a bit bored with all of this convenience, there is nothing like triathlon to add a bit of adventure and spice to your everyday life. Because no matter how much you may want it, you won't be able to get up tomorrow and cover 140.6 miles. You won't be able to do it without a lot of struggle and sacrifice. Indeed you'll most likely have to change your diet, your schedule, your priorities, your mentality, and your body before you can even think about showing up at the starting line.

But I suspect the real secret that many triathletes will eagerly share is that a simpler, easier, and more convenient life...is by no means a better life.

Hidden Secrets

Can you keep a secret? Yes, well the reason that I don't eat French fries is because I'm in training for my next race. It's a secret that I tend to keep to myself, close to me heart and it keeps me smiling and it makes me feel special inside as I look around the restaurant. Sure I want the fries, but I want a personal best in my next race more.

Remote Control

Life has a way of kicking you when you are down…and there's precious little that you can do about it. How do you really battle a tumor or a genetic flaw or a virus or your best friend's diabetes? How do you really fight the good fight when you don't have the tools, skill, knowledge, or experience? How do you control the uncontrollable? You control what little you can and wish and pray for the rest. You get up in the morning and dedicate yourself to climbing this mountain or that for yourself or for your friend or your family.

Why? Because you do have these tools, skills, knowledge, and you can draw on the experience to impose some manner of direct control over this particular mountain. And you hope that you've brought some hope, strength, and joy to this particular day in your life. And perhaps you'll set an example that you can follow for tomorrow's tomorrow when you know that life will again kick you when you are down.

The Joy of Living

The muscle contracts because a signal from the brain travels down a nerve in a fraction of a second. The muscle remembers this move because it has done it time and time again. Indeed it has worked in close harmony with countless other muscles and nerves and arteries and blood cells to propel the body forward. The heart pumps and all over the body hundreds of thousands of miniscule chemical reactions separate and combine atoms and create the energy needed for just this one muscle to move.

It all comes together is a symphony of motion and movement. A perfect balance of fluid dynamics that puts a huge smile on my face as the sweat runs down my nose. This is what it feels like to be completely alive. As my heart pounds in my chest, and my lungs struggle for every atom of air, I know that I've been blessed to be able to use this body to its fullest and best ability. I know the joy of living because I see and feel it in wonderful glorious sweaty Technicolor.

The Agony of Defeat

How do you cheat death? You can't, but you can certainly keep it waiting while you go on with your life. The secret is going on with your life. Because life after all is my suicide mission so that's why I will live it like I know and believe this to be true. I will embrace it for all the joy and pain that it has to offer. I will find my mountains and climb them for my friends, my family, and myself.

I will seek out that which is hard and avoid that which is easy to accomplish. I will forget the convenient and embrace the struggle. I will take joy in this body that God created so perfectly. I will use this body to its fullest potential while God allows me to have the strength and will to do so. And I will keep this an open secret next to my heart. But I will gladly share it with anybody who asks for I always prefer to run with a buddy than run alone This is why I swim, bike, and run.

Why do you tri?

8
Transpiration

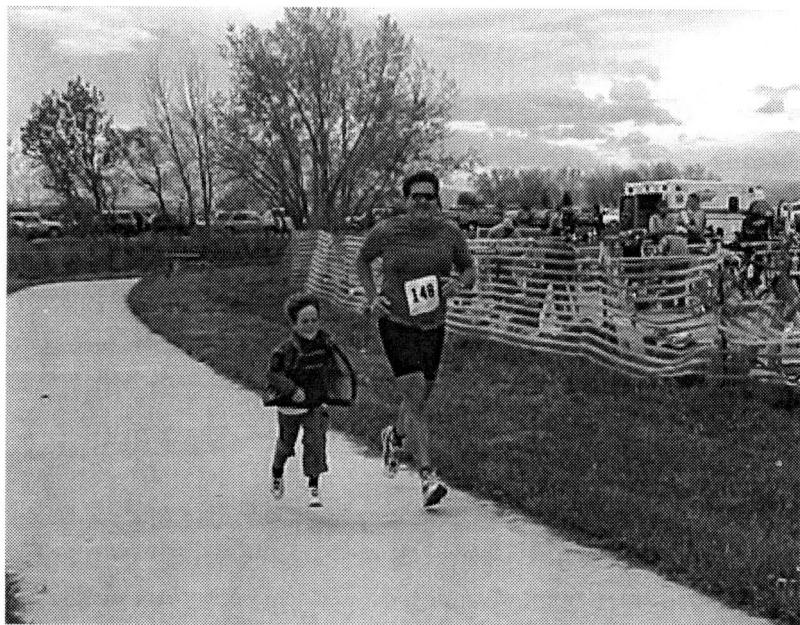

The Secret to Longevity

For the most part I'm a pragmatist, a realist. I don't believe in antidotal evidence. I don't believe in the Loch Ness Monster, or that anybody has ever been abducted by alien's and anally probed, or that Elvis is still alive, or that the Da Vinci Code is anything but clever fiction. But here's something that you may not know about me...I believe in luck. I believe in luck because I have it. I have parking luck. My parking luck is the ability to find a parking space as close as possible to whatever place I'm going. For instance, if I need fish food I'll always get the space just in front of the local PetSmart.

I'd gladly trade my parking luck for lottery luck though, but I don't think that luck can be traded. It's just something that you have or don't have. For instance, one of my best friends, Steve, has sweepstakes luck. Over the last several years he has won trips to Switzerland, Vail, Italy, Puerto Rico, Los Angeles for the Hottest women of Maxim Party, as well as a trip to Mexico for himself and 30 of his best friends. He's also won a full assortment of concert tickets and all kinds of swag like snowboards and golf clubs.

Now you are probably thinking that Steve spends 24/7 entering every sweepstake under the sun. I've asked and he says, "No." What's his secret? He tells me that if he happens to come across a contest that is offering something he likes, he'll enter, but that's it. He won't go out of his way to enter a contest. I know the real reason he wins so much. He has sweepstakes luck.

Speaking of secrets and luck, in a former life I managed a restaurant. One day this large family came in for dinner because they are celebrating a birthday. The patriarch of the family is a spry and diminutive guy who does not look a day over 70. It turns out that he is turning 100 and they are celebrating this huge milestone date.

Here's the sad part, he's currently living with…get this…his daughter's daughter, who is something like 60 herself. He has outlived all his children, and he might just outlive his grandkids. Anyway, as we bring out the blazing birthday cake (image 100 candles) to his table, I make a grand announcement that we have an octogenarian who is turning 100 in front of the entire restaurant. Everybody claps. In fact, as I recall, he even got a standing ovation.

So while all this is going on I lean over to him and whisper, "So what's the secret to living to 100?" He turns to me and with a wry smile he says, "I smoke, I drink, but I don't eat butter."

So there you have it. The secret to longevity is to smoke and drink like a cowboy in a Wild West saloon, but for God's sake keep away from the buttered bread. I suspect that his real secret is that he has longevity luck.

At this point I should confess that I also have another form of luck. One day, about 10 years ago, I was doing my usual half-hour stationary bike ride at the club when I noticed a rather attractive woman on the bike next to me. At the time I had lots of work clients, so I was trying to place her because she looked very familiar. After a while I gave up, but it was then that I noticed the rather burly man in a dark suit standing behind her bike.

It was strange enough to see a big, burly dude in a suit at the health club, but I also happened to notice that his suit jacket was open and exposing a rather large pearl handled gun.

In an instant, it dawned on me that this guy was a bodyguard and that the attractive young woman was Claudia Schiffer. Now it may seem strange to you that Claudia Schiffer was at my health club, but you have to know the rest of the story. I was living in Prague in the Czech Republic at the time and my health club happened to be in the Intercontinental Hotel where Claudia was staying and filming her workout video.

Since that time my celebrity luck has only increased. Here are a few more examples.

- I've had dinner with the boys from U-2,
  - I've bumped into the Rolling Stones,
  - I've played golf with Sean Connery.
  - I've had odd encounters with Hilary Clinton, Sigourney Weaver, Rob Schneider, and even Fabio.

What is an odd encounter you ask? For instance, I was at a local pizza place with an Irish friend when this tall guy in an overcoat walks in. As I'm ordering a pizza, the tall guy asks me what's good. I indicate that I like the vegetarian pizza, to which he says, "Great" and orders one. I sat down and my Irish friend asks, "Do you know who that was?"

"No," I say, "some tall guy in an overcoat."

He says, "No, you dummy - that was Liam Neeson." So now you know that Liam Neeson likes vegetables on his pizza.

Perhaps my celebrity luck was strongest when I walked out to the hot tub at a hotel in Aspen. I noticed that there were three other people in the tub. From behind at least one looked like a pretty attractive woman. I get in, look up, and I'm face to face with a bikini-clad Cindy Crawford. I make some stupid remark about the water being warm. She agrees and I sit down in the tub trying not to stare.

After about 5 minutes she and her friends leave just as two big cigar-huffing Texans are heading into the hot tub.

"Boy, you know who that was?" they say with their jaws wide open.

"Yup, I know who that was" I reply. "I have celebrity luck."

A Triathlete's Christmas

It only seems correct that during the holiday time of the year I take stock and give thanks for all wonders of triathlon (of course from a triathlete's point of view).

I'm Thankful for Chlorine

Now that I spend countless hours at the local pool, swimming back and forth like some caged and deranged zoo animal, I give thanks to modern chemistry. For without it the local youngsters would quickly turn my beloved pool into what the ancient Greeks called the Urinarium.

I'm Thankful for Lycra

This wonderfully modern, stretchy fabric allows all triathletes (men and women) to wear comfortable yet snug and tight fitting clothes over raced tuned bodies.

I'm Thankful for Sunglasses

Not only do they shade my eyes from the sun, but they allow all triathletes to anonymously observe the wonders of tight fitting Lycra over race tuned bodies.

I'm Thankful for Carbon Fiber

Mark, my old biking buddy in high school used to like to say that bike racing is not about the chassis but about the engine... as he kicked my butt on the way back home. Well Mark, thanks to the wonders of carbon fiber it's now all about the chassis. After all, it is so much easier for my bike to shed a few pounds than for me to lose weight.

I'm Thankful for Pull Buoys

Or as I like to call them during an especially hard masters workout in the pool: the poor man's wet suit. They provide all the buoyancy at a fraction of the cost.

I'm Thankful for Big Girls on Mountain Bikes

They keep me honest and grounded and in touch with what's real and what's not. Just when I think that I'm the next Lance, one of these gals will fly by me like I'm standing still and give me a large helping of reality.

I'm Thankful for Fast Food

There's nothing better than a 1,500-plus calorie super-sized meal after an especially hard and long workout. Training for an Ironman not only makes you fit, but it also makes for pure guilt free fast food dining enjoyment.

I'm Thankful for GU

Not only is it a great, quick and fast energy boost supplement, but it also provides that added hand stickiness that makes for superior bike handling through better handlebar grip.

I'm Thankful for Dogs

My dog always gives me a great reason to go for a run. She always loves to go for a run with me...no matter what time of day or night, no matter what kind of weather, no matter what she's doing or not doing, and no matter how good or bad I feel, a run with her always makes me feel better.

I'm Thankful for OLN

The Outdoor Life Network now broadcasts most Ironman races as well as many of the ITU races. Much of the time the production values of these broadcast are so poor that their goofy race coverage will certainly keep our sport a small and well hidden treasure.

I'm Thankful for the Finish Line

I don't really need to explain this one, do I?

I'm Thankful for Body Glide

I don't really need to explain this one, do I?

I'm Thankful for Beer

I don't really need to explain this one, do I?

I'm Thankful for Aero Bars

Aero Bars have become the surest and quickest way to identify fellow triathletes on a training ride.

I'm Thankful for Traditional Water Bottle Holders

The new water bottle holders, located behind bike seats that are now all the rage, have almost cost me my life twice. Why…because they also double as missile launchers when the guy in front hits a bump.

I'm Thankful for the Swim

It keeps the run weasels honest.

I'm Thankful for the Run

It keeps the swim weasels honest.

I'm Thankful for the Bike

It's a great way to dry off before the run.

Finally, I'm Thankful for the Sport of Triathlon

It's a great way to be alive.

The Magic Moments of Racing

I watched the new version of King Kong when it was first released. At over three hours, it soon became one of those movies where you keep checking your watch to see how much longer until the end.

But that wasn't my real problem with the film. It was Ann Darrow's (played by Naomi Watts) teeth. They kept changing colors. At the beginning of the film, which takes place during the depression, they were somewhat gray and lack luster. On the boat to Skull Island they radiated a white unearthly glow. On the island, when she was terrified of King Kong, they went back to their dull grayish color. And of course at the end of the film, on top of the Empire State building during her close up as the sun is rising over New York, her teeth were so white I almost had to put on my sunglasses. It is during moments like this that the magic spell of the movie is broken. When I can clearly see the heavy hand of the filmmaker I lose interest and check my watch.

The same thing happens when I'm watching a movie and there's a car scene. Predictably, the filmmakers remove the headrest from the front seats so you can better see the actors when they shoot the scene from behind. No matter what the actors are saying or doing, I'm thinking to myself, "What the hell happened to the headrest?" Or "Who would buy a car without a headrest?"

The movie magic is broken and I'm checking my watch. Have you noticed that the same thing can happen during a race? One second you are completely living in the moment, and the next second something happens and the race seems to go on without you.

This certainly happened to me was when I flatted eight times during my last Iron distance race. The first two flats were fixed since I had two spares, but by the third flat the magic was broken. I sat on the side of the road watching the other athletes zoom by, and I knew I was on the outside looking in at the race. This also happened to me during this year's Boulder Peak Triathlon when a swimmer died in the wave just before mine. The magic was broken.

From these and a few other races I learned an important lesson that changed my definition of winning. I used to believe that winning was either **a)** winning the race or my age group, or **b)** achieving a preset goal or personal best. Don't get me wrong; these are still important to me, but not as important as they once used to be.

I've come to realize that my definition of winning is how I deal with that moment when the magic is broken or, in other words, how I react when things don't go my way. I suppose I learned this lesson because over the years I worked my way up the food chain from sprint to Iron distance races. The chances of things going wrong in a longer race are obviously greater, as there is more time for them to head south.

This does not mean that you won't have problems in a sprint race. I recall a local sprint race my wife did a few years ago where she had just gotten a road bike. Before then we both raced on our mountain bikes, which are pretty sturdy beasts and tend not to break so easily. She climbed on the bike and started to peddle up the first hill when her chain fell off. Being new to road bikes and in the heat of battle, she began what to her seemed like an eternal battle to get the chain back on. This battle with the bike raged back and forth as she fought to replace the chain. It culminated in a long string of expletives that would make an old Turkish sailor blush, yet eventual victory on her part. Only then did she happen to look up and see the completely open-mouthed and stunned young family of spectators trying to enjoy their Sunday morning.

It is how I deal with the magic moments of racing that defines winning and losing for a Clydesdale like me. You don't have to flat or endure a mechanical breakdown to experience a magical moment. It happens all the time…especially on the swim and run. Let's face it, it's pretty easy to be in the moment when all is going well, when you feel fine, and the race gods are with you. But what happens when somebody accidentally kicks you in the face at the start of the race and knocks off your goggles? This almost happened to Joanna Zeiger at this year's Ironman Brazil, except that her goggles stayed on while her nose ended up broken. Even with a broken nose she managed to win the race.

Or what happens when that wetsuit that you borrowed is too tight. This happened to my neighbor during an open water swim a few years ago. What did she do? She actually peeled off her wetsuit *in the water*, gave it to a lifeguard, and kept swimming. This must be some kind of feat of magic because I can barely remove my wetsuit on dry land.

How about when things go south on the run? I'm sure you've had cramps and the usual stomach issues. But how about Tim DeBoom passing a kidney stone? That actually happened to him during the Kona world championships. I was watching the race as he was vying for the lead. One moment he was running a 5-minute mile and the next moment he was in an ambulance on the way to the hospital. Can you image the pain of passing a kidney stone *during* an Ironman race? Now if that won't break the magic of the race moment, nothing will.

Why Bowling is Better than Triathlon

The other day I went bowling for the first time in about 10 years and was amazed at how the sport has changed. If you have not gone bowling in a few years, you may want to give it a fresh try.

It is with a bit of sadness that I announce that I have officially changed sports. I have seen the light and that light shines down with a soft shimmer onto the gleaming polished floors of your neighborhood bowling alley. I've discovered that bowling is much better than triathlon, and here's why:

A) Bowling Babes It used to be that bowling had the image of being...let's say...for the endurance challenged. We'll not anymore. Today's new generation of bowlers is not only hip and fit, but also scantily clad. Forgot those skimpy triathlon shorts and tops that some gals like to wear when they race. The bowling bikini is in and it makes triathlon wear look almost prudish by comparison.

B) Beer What do you get after an extremely long day on your local Iron distance course? A bottle of water and a kick in the ass to get out of the finish line area as soon as possible. Not with bowling. You don't have to swim/bike/run some 140 miles to get lousy beer. At your local bowling alley the beer is just a short stumble from the field of competition. In fact beer flows so freely that many of today's top competitors start drinking long before the competition ever starts.

C) Early Mornings I'm getting a wee bit tired of all the predawn workouts. I find myself stumbling out of bed just to dive into a chilly swimming pool just to be able get out in a hurry just so I can make it to work on time.

Do you have any idea at what time your local bowling alley opens? No? Well neither do I, but I have a strong suspicion that it opens sometime around lunchtime. And unlike triathlon there's really not much training you can do without an open bowling alley. I could be wrong about that as you can certainly do 12-ounce curls at home. Bowling just keeps getting better.

D) Equipment   There's soooo much *stuff* you need to be a triathlete. The bike gear alone can run into several thousands of dollars. Now add in all of your running and swimming *stuff*, plus coaching, plus books and videotapes on this and that, and you have just reached your average credit card limit. On the other hand a perfectly fine bowling ball runs about $50. And that still leaves lots of cash for beer.

E) Food   Let's face it—most of us secretly love a big heaping plate of nachos with steak, beans, and sour cream. Or how about a healthy pile of lightly browned crispy fries with a side of tangy catsup? Have you ever tried eating nachos on the bike or fries on the run? Well I have, and I can tell you they get cold really fast.

F) Weather   The weather in your typical bowling alley is a constant and totally comfortable temperature that encourages your typical bowling babe to attend. There are no wind, rain, cold, ice, snow, mean dogs, or crazy drivers. Okay, there may be crazy drivers, but their cars are in the parking lot and their car keys are safely in their pockets.

G) Sports Injuries   It is very difficult to hurt yourself bowling. You could always drop the ball on your foot, but this, I have been well informed, is something that happens very rarely. Better yet, unlike triathlon were those seat mounted bottle rockets (water bottles mounted behind the seat and that

that come flying out at the first bump and get caught in my wheels) are becoming the norm, most bowling competitors rarely bowl the wrong way.

H) Fashion   We all know that bowling shoes and shirts are in vogue right now. Some of the world's top fashion houses have styled beautiful shoes and clothes that are considered bowling alley chic from New York to Paris.

On the other hand you won't turn many heads with your old sweaty and stinky Nike sweats. You will turn heads with your low cut Speedos but in a "man look at that hairy European dad" sort of way.

I) Training   For the most part training is totally pointless in bowling, which of course saves countless hours for more productive activity like watching television. If you do feel the need to train, bowling requires only one arm. Thus your training regiment can be completely exclusive to your bowling arm. I suggest 12-ounce curls, or 24-ounce curls for the more advance competitors.

Well, that's why I've decided to switch to bowling. I hope to see you around at the local bowling alley. Did I mention the Bowling Babes? They not only seem to love the sport but also each other. Viva la Bowling!

How to Lose Weight Fast

I've always wanted to write a book called "How to Lose Weight Fast." The book would only have three chapters:

1) Eat Less

2) Exercise More

3) Maintain

Because it really is that simple...or is it? Of course it's not! Weight loss is one of the hardest things to do in today's modern society. We are constantly bombarded with enticing food advertising, not to mention hundreds of quick, easy and cheap eating opportunities.

My mother, like so many others, has spent her entire life fighting the good fight, and for the most part losing the war. I wish I had stock in Jenny Craig, for when she's on the program the company's profits must sore.

Why is it that so many of us fight the battle of the bulge and lose every time? Logically we all know what must be done (eat less and exercise more) and yet we try the newest diets, eat the newest low-cal foods, and go to all kinds of extremes to shed the increasing pounds.

I really need to add a few chapters to my book. Two to be exact:

4) Be Honest

5) Stay Motivated

I find that when I'm trying to lose weight I turn into one massive liar, and I develop an ability to rationalize that would make Kirstie Alley proud. What's worse, the harder I try to lose weight, the more I lie to myself. I come up with all sorts of rationalizations for my poor eating habits like, "I just ran for half an hour so I can eat this peanut butter cup, and oh what the heck, the other one as well. And I might as well wash it all down with a Coke since I just burned all those calories running."

But it gets worse. When I'm really working hard to lose weight I'll rationalize my poor diet with the expectation of a heavy workout. For instance I'll do things like, "It's okay to have this burger and fries and a chocolate shake for lunch since I'll be going for an extra long swim tonight." The problem is that by "tonight" I get tired and that extra long swim turns into an extra long nap.

To help me stay honest, I've put together a little cheat sheet that translates caloric intake into the actual amount of time needed to burn those calories. It's kinda like Deal-a-Meal (the weight loss card program that lets you choose foods by mixing and matching cards), except that it lets you eat empty calories based on how much work it will take to actually burn them off.

For instance, the below-mentioned lunch at my favorite burger joint is about 1,700 calories:

Burger: 600
Fries: 400
Shake 700
Total lunch 1,700 Calories

Now this may seem like a lot, but my favorite local hamburger place is Red Robin and their burgers and shakes are big and their fries are bottomless. Remember we're being totally honest.

So how much exercise do I need to do to burn off my lunch?

2.0 hours of swimming at 1:15 per 100 yards, which is fast for me, so I figure 2.5 hours for me.

2:00 hours of biking at 20 mph, which is also fast for me, so I figure about 2:30 hours of biking for me.

1:15 hours of running at an 8:00 minutes per mile pace, again fast for me, so I figure 1:30 of running for me.

You can use the following as a calorie burning rule of thumb:

700 calories an hour of constant swimming
700 calories an hour of intermediate biking
(figure 19-25 mph)
1,100 calories an hour of easy running
(9-10 mph)

Therefore, if you have a 12 ounce can of coke (140 calories) plus a \chocolate Hershey bar (130 calories) as a snack you better figure on spending a half an hour on the bike or in the pool just to burn off that 5 minute snack.

When I look at it this way, I begin to wonder if that snack is really worth all the effort. And the problem, of course, is that I'm assuming that I'll actually do the work. If I get lazy I'm in trouble. Watching Television burns about 100 calories an hour.

That means that if I go to Red Robin for lunch tomorrow, I'll have to watch 17 hours of television to just stay at no weight gain. Or I could always type on this computer for 10 hours (typing on a computer burns about 170 calories an hour) to get that much needed work out.

Ironman or Ironfit ?

You spent your entire year (or is it life?) training to get to this one precious moment in time. The first time you saw it on television you were amazed and bit mystified as to why people would spend so much time and effort for this single moment. As time passed and you had some success in your racing, you began to better understand the significance of this moment and perhaps dream of one day hearing those magic words, "Your Name,....you are an Ironman!" And then you're an Ironman. Now what?

You'll probably spend the next two days eating and sleeping and replaying the day's events in your mind. You're likely to always remember how good and salty that warm chicken broth tasted on the last few miles of your marathon. You'll most likely never forget how hard it was to start a marathon after the 112-mile bike ride. How heavy and tired your legs felt, and how you could not even image running for the next four to six hours as the sunset and the day transitioned into night.

You'll remember the early morning start as you walked into the water full of nervous tension knowing that you "only" had 140.6 miles to go before you were done. Will you recall looking around at the other faces as they looked back into your eyes wondering the same thing?

Or perhaps you'll remember the salty taste of your own sweat as it rolled down your forehead, over your nose and onto your lips as you peddled away in the aero position for 112 miles. Or will you remember how you had to force down that 10th GU or 5th Powerbar, even though your stomach clearly gagged at the mere thought of eating?

Will you recall all those straining faces that you passed or that passed you? Will you remember the kind hands of all the great volunteers who handed you more food and drink as you just kept going…even though your body and mind were screaming at you to stop?

You'll probably tell your friends and family that you finished in this or that many hours, and hopefully they will be impressed. They probably won't really get it, as they weren't there with you on those countless early morning hours in the pool. Or on those long century rides, or lonely 18-mile training runs on cold Saturday mornings. But you'll always know the pain and the pleasure, the very high highs and the bottomless lows, the terror and the boundless joy, and that's what really matters in the end. And now what?

I have a really sweet little secret I'll be happy to share with you. For me being an Ironman isn't really all that important. Sure it may be the cherry on top of the cake, but the real treat is being Ironfit. I walk around all day with this sweet little secret that I know, keep to myself, and treasure. It's not something that I tell people because the telling is not important. The knowing is what's really important.

For instance, I know that I can run 14 miles at a drop of a hat and not feel all that tired or even winded. I know this because I just did it the other day and I felt so great afterwards that I even raced a short indoor tri the next day.

I think back to just a few short years ago, when the thought of running 10k, or 6.2 miles, seemed like a huge achievement. Every year I would train long and hard to run the local 10k race, and afterwards it seemed like I had just climbed Mount Everest.

And of course running a 10k race still is a great achievement, but from my Ironfit perspective a 10k is an easy mid-week run. This doesn't make me any better of person; it just makes me happy and warm inside to know that I've come such a long way.

For instance, I know that I can swim 10k today. I know this because a few years ago I did it as part of an open water long course race when I was in worse shape than I am now. By the way, I have a funny story from that race.

Open water swim rules don't allow you to wear a wetsuit, or anything other than a swimsuit and goggles. You also get a support boat. You're allowed to eat and drink, but you can't hold onto the boat or touch the bottom when you stop swimming to take on nutrition. This means that your support person can throw you food and drinks, but you can't touch the boat to get them. I thought that I was being really clever when I invented my swimming nutrition buoy.

Basically, I duct taped a Gatorade and Ice Tea bottle on a pull buoy and tied a rope around the entire thing. This way, or so I thought, my support person could throw me the drinks and pull them back with the rope. This part worked. Unfortunately, I had never tested my nutrition buoy. The first time I tried to drink the Gatorade, I immediately began to sink, and of course let go of the bottle top, leaving me with no way to close the bottle. When my crew pulled it back to the boat, I had a new Gatorade formula that was half Gatorade and half dirty lake water.

But I digress; I did eventually finish the swim a bit dehydrated in just over 4 hours. The good news is that the thought of a "mere" 2.4-mile swim today seems like a walk in the park.

And in a way that's really the point to being Ironfit. It means that I know I can swim, bike, or run a pretty crazy distance and not feel tired or worn out. More importantly, I think, no... I know, that it also means that I have more energy and drive in the other parts of my daily life. It has become a lifestyle choice for me because I get so much more out of it than I put into it. I could spend 10 hours a week watching television or reading a book, but instead I spend it swimming, biking and running. And the really great trick is that I still have time to read, write, and watch television.

Why? Because I spend a lot less time being sick, because I sleep better, because I eat better, because I can concentrate better at work, because my mind stays sharp, and my emotions stay level, and because I get so much more joy out of life that I have so much more I can share.

So now what?

My next race is Ironman Austria (summer 2006), but really, between you and me, I'm looking more forward to the journey than to the destination.

9
Race Reviews

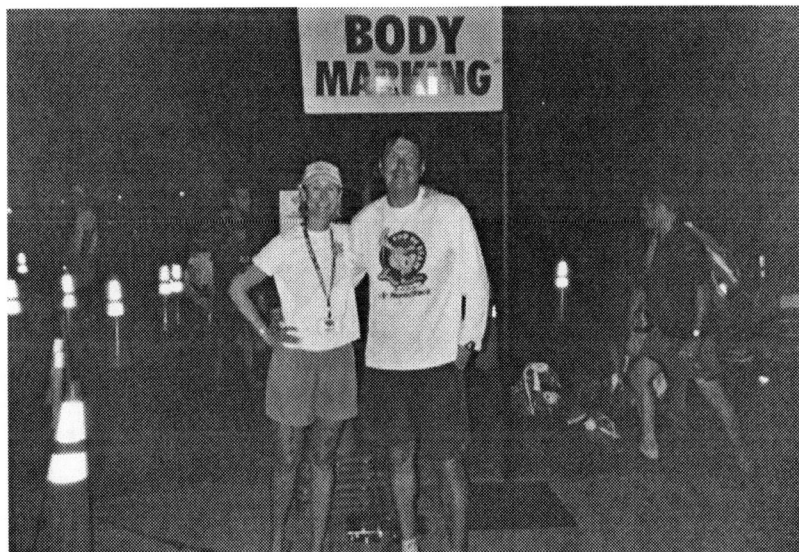

Canyonlands Half Marathon

Everyman Rating
No Brewski (It is in Utah after all)

Rating Scale (based on the amount of beer needed after race)
- 4 Brewskis: So excruciatingly painful and lame you'll need a full year of recovery just to forget this race
- 3 Brewskis: The best thing said (and remembered) about race is, "I finished."
- 2 Brewskis: A challenging race in a masochistic, "I could do it again" sort-of-way given enough time and Ibuprofen
- 1 Brewski: Good solid race that exceeds your expectations
- No Brewski: A must-do annual event for both friends and family

The Race
http://moabhalfmarathon.org

If the race organizers were to set up several dozen treadmills down the main street of Moab and set them to 13 miles and call it the race, I think I would still go. There is a reason this race is 31-years-old with a lottery to get in. The reason is that this is a spectacularly well-run race, in a beautiful location, with perfect weather, and a gently rolling downhill course that almost guarantees to help you smash your personal best.

Move closer to the page, please. This part is just between you and me. You see I'm really having a hard time writing this review because I sort of feel like I want to keep this race our little secret. I've been lucky enough to get into the race two years in a row and all I need is for the word to get out that this race just rocks! So do me a small favor please. Let's just keep the rest of this review between us. Call it our little secret and if you do happen to enter the race and get a slot just smile and keep it to yourself. Okay, now that we've got that cleared up, here's the rest of the review. Feel free to move back now.

The Location

What makes this race so incredible is the location. The race starts about 10 miles up the canyon from Moab. The course follows the road down along the silt filled roaring Colorado River as it cuts through the red clay earth creating towering cliffs of almost indescribable beauty. But I'll give it a shot anyway.

The massive towering cliffs loom over you as you pound the rolling pavement toward Moab. Image yourself running a half marathon in a Vatican Cathedral or perhaps through the very opening of the Grand Canyon. There is a spiritual timeless beauty to this part of the country that is real and palatable. You can almost feel the wondering ghost of the countless Anastasi Indians that made this part of the Southwest their home.

There is actually a stone on the other side of Moab called the birthing stone that still carries the scars of long dead Anastasi Indian women. These now forgotten women clutched the rock while giving birth and clawed their hand marks into the stone during their labor spasm.

The Racers

The two largest age groups by far are females 25 to 29 and 30 to 34. It's hard to image a larger gathering of blonde fit and trim females outside of a Berlin rave party. If you are a single Mormon guy, this must be the very best place to pick up your next wife or two. Not only are your pickings extremely fit, but also Moab seems to actually have some of the most relaxed alcohol rules in all of Utah. During race weekend you might actually have a chance at getting a tipsy post race prospect!

Moab

Just like with Germany, I have a deep love/hate relationship with Utah. In Germany I love all the "everything in order" mentality and really hate the "everything in order " mentality. Utah, on the other hand, strikes me as the 1950's America of my sitcom dreams where family values still rule the roost, and you can get as much ice cold Coke as you'd like as long as you completely forget about the rum.

Moab has best of both worlds. It has that great family friendly attitude plus two breweries. The half marathon with some 3,000 racers and their friends and family is by far the biggest weekend event in this tiny town. Yet the locals really put out the welcome mats and are genuinely happy to have the race in their town. Everybody we met bent over backwards to accommodate our little Boulder band of runners.

Swag

One particular year the race organizers did away with the traditional Kokopelli finisher medals, and instead spent the money on high quality running shirts and hats. I personally can't stand another cotton race shirt or running hat, so it was great to get something I will actually use again and not give away to my brother-in-law.

Support

Here's a tip to all you "would be race organizers" from the Moab crew. Have your water and Gatorade ready and stacked up for the runners. Place signs a few hundred feet in front of the water stations letting the runners know they're just ahead. This allows me to pop a GU just before the aid station and grab a water or Gatorade to wash it down with and not miss a step. At too many other races they have clumsy kids filling up the cups with tepid water in tiny amounts just seconds before I go by.

The Weather

For the two years that I've run the race the temperatures have been almost perfect—between the fifties and sixties. One year we had an almost constant headwind, but it mostly served to keep me cool.

NTKS (Need To Know Secrets)

The race starts at 10:00 a.m., which is Godsend for all of us non-morning people. The buses transport you up to the start of the race starting at about 7:00, but you can hang out in your hotel until at least 9:00 a.m. and catch the last bus. No need to freeze in the Canyon listening to that mandatory seventies pre-race hard rock. I get it guys, but I'm not runnin' on empty.

When you get to the start of the race, walk down to the river until they call you to the line. Not only is the sand soft, making for a great place to sit and stretch, but the sun will be shining over the canyon cliffs onto this beach keeping you warn and cozy.

After the race I like to have a chocolate shake at the Moab Diner. This is a brief walk down Main Street. They still make their shakes the old fashioned way. Image, if you will, someone actually still using vanilla ice cream, milk, and chocolate syrup. If you are feeling really giddy, consider adding a hamburger and fries for just over $5.00. You've gotta love the 1950's prices.

After the race, stick around an extra day or two and visit Arches National Park or Island in the Sky at Canyons National Park. Both of these spectacular national gems are just minutes outside of Moab. I could blabber on about how beautiful they are, but you just take my word for it and check them out for yourself as part of your next perfect family race weekend.

Great Floridian Triathlon XV

Everyman Rating
2.5 Brewskis

Rating Scale (based on the amount of beer needed after race)
- 4 Brewskis: So excruciatingly painful and lame you'll need a full year of recovery just to forget this race
- 3 Brewskis: The best thing said (and remembered) about race is, "I finished."
- 2 Brewskis: A challenging race in a masochistic, "I could do it again" sort-of-way given enough time and Ibuprofen
- 1 Brewski: Good solid race that exceeds your expectations
- No Brewski: A must-do annual event for both friends and family

The Race

www.sommersports.com/events/greatfloridian

Here's a funny story. The police delayed the start of the 2005 race by about half an hour. It seems there were three cars parked in the parking lot, which served as the run up to the transition area. The police felt it was unsafe to have these cars "parked" there as they might pounce in front of hapless racers. I remembered this odd start some 14 hours later as I was running in the pitch-black Florida night, into oncoming traffic, on a road with no shoulder, wearing only a spaghetti thin neon glow tube. Thank God they held up the race start and put orange cones around those cars. They may have belonged to somebody who might have left early and ran over me on the run.

The Great Floridian Triathlon is really three races in one. There is an Iron distance race, a half Iron distance race, and some sort of super-sprint, which I assume is very short.

The Great Floridian Triathlon is also the national long course championship. I'm not really sure, and nor were most of the racers, what the international long course distance is, but the winners in each age group can go to the International Championships in Australia and find out.

I raced the full Iron distance, and I kept seeing the half Iron competitors. They were the ones passing me on the bike. My wife was happy to have the company of several hundred half competitors. I, on the other hand, grew tired of constantly being passed by these half weasels that only had to do one 57-mile loop.

I suspect the race organizers need to have three races to make this a viable event. But they ought to at least have enough water for those of us on the second loop of the bike.

The Racers

There are a lot of the old-school types still doing this race. You know, the kind who have been racing for the last 15 years and still wear those shin high red stripped socks with some funky old-school Puma running shoes that might actually be hip again if they were worn by somebody 30 years younger.

There are also a lot of great people in this race. I cannot say enough good things about the racers that I met before, during, and after the race. A huge shout has to go out to the Iron Penguin who raced this course too many times to count, and who organized a pre-race inspection of the run and bike courses. Dude, you are great! From now on just call me the Iron Dumpling.

There was also a large group of Brazilian racers from Miami who made the race very interesting by their bravado and considerable lack of clothing. There was a fun group from Chicago who swept many of the awards and, unfortunately, wore way too much clothing.

There was our small band of racers from Colorado, who had the huge advantage of altitude, which was off set by the huge disadvantage of heat and humidity.

And, of course, no one will forget Wilma, who thankfully showed up a day later, but never-the-less managed to spawn a few tornadoes right on the race course. Thank goodness we were able to watch her from the safety of our hotel room in Orlando the day after the race.

The Swim

The swim consists of two long triangles through the murky waters of Lake Minneola. And when I say murky, I mean this water is so black that you can't see your hand in it as you swim. The race organizers blamed this dark water on the natural tanins in the lake. I suppose swimming in the dark water is like swimming in a fine Merlot.

A nice touch on the swim was the water station between the two loops. And unlike the bike, there was no swimming uphill.

Transitions

Transition areas were well manned with very cheerful and very helpful volunteers. Once you figured-out the dizzying number of bags and what to put in them, you are set to race. The half Iron weasels didn't get in the way too much, but the changing tents were extremely hot. I felt bad for the volunteers who had to staff them all day expect for the dude who took my water. I asked for a cup of water as I was changing into my run clothes. The "helpful" volunteer ran right up to the cooler, got a cup, poured a large cup of icy-cold water, and drank it.

The Bike

The bike course consists of two 57-mile loops in and around Clermont. Now I know that two 57-mile loops added together equal 114 miles and not the "proper" 112 miles. But that's what my bike computer said and others confirmed it, like the Iron Penguin, so I'm sticking with it. Never argue with the Iron Penguin.

The bike course is not flat, and boy this is an understatement. If you want a flat course, I suggest you try Ironman Florida, which has one hill, which also happens to be a bridge.

The Great Floridian is similar to IM Wisconsin. Worse yet the race organizers like to put the hills around every right turn. Oh look there's a right turn. It must mean I'll be *out* of my saddle again.

The big hill is called Sugarloaf, which comes the second time around at about mile 95 into the race. The good news is this hill allows you to really stretch your sore legs by walking up a 13 percent grade. Just bring plenty of water because there was none at the tail end of the bike. Those half weasels drank it all on first loop. Did I mention I was constantly being passed on the first loop?

The Run

The run is a 10k out-and-back and three 7ish mile loops around the lake. It is almost entirely flat, unless you consider the massive sideways camber of the road a hill. You should, as it really hurts to run on this road. But than again you have no choice, as there is no shoulder.

Some of the high points of my run included the snarling Pit Bulls that provided extra incentive for a wining time, and running by myself in the pitch black night past several unmanned aid stations.

There is, however, one of those huge searchlights at the finish line, the kind that car dealers seem to favor. It illuminates the evening sky with glorious rotating lights. It calls to you in a teasing sort of way—"Come here and be done mon ami. Oh… but you are only on lap one, no no no—you must go back into the murky night."

NTKS (Need To Know Secrets)

- The "mandatory" marathon at the end of the race seems very voluntary indeed. Nobody checked my number at the end of the out and back part of the run, and nobody counted the loops but me. And no there were no timing mats on the run. I suspect a few competitors may have set a "personal best" on the run.

- There is a famous aid station on the run manned by the mad dogs. This is a must stop aid station as these folks know how to party. In fact, all the volunteers along the race were great. Thanks to them for their encouragement. Without them it would be a much harder race, as there is no crowd support along the racecourse.

- There was a second great aid station this particular year manned by the Flintstones. These were folks dressed up as characters from the Flintstones cartoon. Get it: Wilma. The women of this aid station were especially out going since they seemed to have been drinking a wee bit. On every loop they become friendlier and friendlier offering hugs, and dare I say even a kiss or two of the French kind.

- There are great big trophies for the top ten places in each age group. I actually got a great big trophy, as I took 7th in my category. And hey, nobody but us has to know that there were only eight Clydesdale competitors.

Florida Half Ironman

Everyman Rating
3 Brewskis

Rating Scale (based on the amount of beer needed after race)
- 4 Brewskis: So excruciatingly painful and lame you'll need a full year of recovery just to forget this race
- 3 Brewskis: The best thing said (and remembered) about race is, "I finished."
- 2 Brewskis: A challenging race in a masochistic, "I could do it again" sort-of-way given enough time and Ibuprofen
- 1 Brewski: Good solid race that exceeds your expectations
- No Brewski: A must-do annual event for both friends and family

The Race
http://www.floridahalfironman.com

If you like the combination of extreme heat, humidity, and Mickey Mouse, this race is for you! This is certainly one of the most family friendly races on the triathlete's calendar. While you sweat and toil assembling your bike, the rest of the family can be out having lunch in Germany or France at Epcot Center, or perhaps a more exotic African fare at Disney's Animal Kingdom.

While you sit in the blazing sun at the pre-race meeting, the kids can be frolicking at the nearby beach. And while you race through the bike unfriendly streets of Disney's back lot, the family can be sipping a cool lemonade or iced tea at Fort Wilderness. However, all this family-fun does come with a price…a very hefty price. I'm now a complete believer in the Disney business plan. They have perfected the art of maxing-out your credit cards with a smile and a song. (In my case it was the two hour Hoop-Dee-Doo Music Review which came to something a bit over $200 for my small family.) Indeed, the hardest part of this entire race is opening the credit card statement upon your return home.

The Racers

I asked the super buff guy at the pool where he got his rub on Ironman tattoo, which was prominently blazing red in the mid-day sun. He gave me a look of total disregard contempt and said in a heavy French accent, "This is not a child's tattoo. She is real!"

I considered this for a while and decided that while I certainly use many fine products and services daily, the thought of tattooing myself with a corporate logo of their manufacturer was a bit much. Can you image the conversation with your spouse? "Honey the dishwasher does such a great job that I just added a Whirlpool tattoo to my left shoulder."

"That's great dear, it just looks super above your Volvo and American Express tattoos. I'm getting my Playtex tattoo done tomorrow."

By now you may have guessed that many of the racers are the Ironman hardcore international types. Not to be out done, many of the local racers are also the hardcore Ironman types. I met another guy from Wisconsin who had a tattoo (real) of every Ironman race he had completed. For instance, the Wisconsin race featured a prominent smiling cow above the Ironman tattoo while the Florida full Ironman featured a happy leaping porpoise.

The Swim

The swim is a lop-sided triangle. Athletes start in about 20 waves. As usual, the Clydesdales and Athenas started in one of the very last waves. Note 1 to race organizers: we are getting a bit tired of always being last. Is there a secret race director manual that says that Clydesdales and Athenas must start last because they will drink all the beer? Do race organizers get a secret thrill in seeing us big boys struggle through the mid-day heat while all the pro's and small girls have long ago finished the race?

Except for the rumors of triathlete eating alligators, the swim is very pleasant. The course is well marked. The water is warm, not wetsuit legal. There is only one big loop, which means you won't get caught up in many elbow battles. Enjoy the clear water and keep an eye out for fish in the shallow parts.

Transition

Note 2 to Organizers: Black Astroturf like carpet is a really bad idea in Florida.

The transition is on a beach and the Ironman folks had kindly covered most of the beach in black carpet. It felt great to walk on and run on in the morning while putting our stuff into transition. I loved the feeling of soft sand covered by soft carpet. The same cannot be said later in the day. A crash course in hot coal walking would certainly have been helpful during the first and second transition. We were all jumping around like kangaroos trying get our feet into the bike shoes.

The Bike

The bike course winds its way through the back lots of Disney until racers hit the mean streets of Orlando and the country roads farther out. Friendly Disney security guards cheer racers on as they fly through their property. It would have been more helpful if they actually stopped the traffic. At one point a bunch of us big guys were almost taken out by a sleepy-eyed Disney employee who mistook the racecourse for his own personal highway. He came at us head-on in an old Dodge. He didn't seem to be bothered a bit by the bikes that were flying left and right to avoid a head on collision.

The other unpleasant surprise is how hilly the bike course gets in the middle. Who thinks of big hills when they think of Florida? Not me until I had to get out of my seat as the road turned up and continued to climb for a half mile at a time.

It was then that I also noticed that it was getting a wee bit hot and muggy. I usually can't tell when I'm sweating on the bike. Climbing the hills in the mid-day Florida heat, I was more like Sponge Bob than Simon Lessing, who won the race, and whom I was sure was already done as I headed back to the transition area for a second round of coal walking.

The Run

The run on this course was changed in 2005 to two loops in and out of the Fort Wilderness Disney property after many complaints about the old Golf Course segment. The good news is that the part of the run that meanders through the shady tree-lined Disney property is great. The bad news is that the part of the run that winds through the semi-trailer parking lot, the hot asphalt bus and RV choked main road entrance to Fort Wilderness, and the dusty and rutted path that follows the dry channel back to the property really sucks.

It especially sucks when it is well above 90 degrees with 100 percent humidity and not a cloud in the sky to provide any shade. It especially, especially sucks when you hit the first aid station back on the property and some well-meaning volunteer hands you a cup of coffee hot Coke. Now that's the type of sensory overload memory that will stick with you for a while.

NTKS (Need To Know Secrets)

- If you are really sick of the heat on the run, the siren call of the finish line may just be too strong to resist. It is only a matter of making a right instead of a left, and you've just finished the run in record time by avoiding that "mandatory" second loop.

- Compared to the Chicago Triathlon the transition area is actually pretty small, but just wait until you start out on the bike. Make sure you know how to run in your bike shoes. You'll have to run through the transition, make a right, run over a bridge, make a left, run down a path, make another turn, and run down a road until you get to the point where you can actually get on the bike. Figure that you might as well add a mile or two to the half marathon while pushing a bike.

- Beware of hot Coke. It kinda tastes like defeat.

- Note 3 to organizers. The best part of the race is having your family at the finish. It is almost worth the heat, humidity and warm Coke.

Accenture Chicago Triathlon Review

Everyman Rating
2 Brewskis

Rating Scale (based on the amount of beer needed after race)
- 4 Brewskis: So excruciatingly painful and lame you'll need a full year of recovery just to forget this race
- 3 Brewskis: The best thing said (and remembered) about race is, "I finished."
- 2 Brewskis: A challenging race in a masochistic, "I could do it again" sort-of-way given enough time and Ibuprofen
- 1 Brewski: Good solid race that exceeds your expectations
- No Brewski: A must-do annual event for both friends and family

The Race
http://www.chicagotriathlon.com

From the official Chicago Triathlon website, "With over 7,500 participants and 100,000 spectators, the Accenture Chicago Triathlon is known as the world's largest triathlon. This year (2005) it will become official with an attempt to set a World Record for the World's Largest Triathlon."

Large certainly best describes this race. As in large transition area (think solider field- sized). Huge distance between the swim exit and the transition (think the average daily jog for a beginner runner). Big holes and bumps on Lake Shore Drive on the bike course (you'll come to understand why many racers are using full-suspension mountain bikes). A long wait before the start (you could finish the entire race in the time spent waiting for your wave start). Huge lines for the few available porta-potties. This could also officially be the world's largest quadathlon testing not only swimming, biking, and running but also intestinal fortitude and Olympic caliber bladder control.

The Racers

The typical field consists of a highly explosive mixture of newbies, weekend warriors, and hardcore pro wannabes. From the rapid to the rotund to the rowdy, this race has it all. Running to the finish in 2004, I saw several guys who looked like they had a very up close and personal view of Lake Shore Drive (LSD). On a positive note, they seemed proud of their road rash as an exclusive souvenir of having finished the race.

The Swim

Imagine putting about 250 race ready athletes into your neighborhood swimming pool and you've got the start of the Chicago Triathlon. The swim consists of two swim lanes that run along the Monroe Street Harbor sea wall and make up the Olympic distance swim. This is an especially great race for all of those who have perfected the art of swimming over/under/ through other swimmers as huge splashing waves of racers enter the water every few minutes. A very talented swimmer could potentially swim the entire race on the backs of others. I found open water for about two minutes before I hit the next wave of slower swimmers. I also had to find a good doctor after the race for a nasty ear infection I got from the lake water. You've been warned.

Transition

You know how some people like to bring a balloon to mark their bikes in transition. You might consider finding one of those novelty stores that sells life-sized balloons of Dumbo because anything smaller will just get lost in transition. Imagine the long-term parking lot at O'Hare Airport on the Wednesday before Thanksgiving, but with bikes instead of cars, and you've got the image. Word to the wise: In 2004 it was a bit on the windy side (and by bit I mean freaking hurricane conditions), as befits the windy city. I think some racers over did it with their balloons. I swear I saw what looked like several LiteSpeed bikes high above Lake Michigan well on their way to Canada.

The Bike

The Olympic distance bike course consist of two loops up and down LSD if and when you have managed to negotiate your way through transition. This is the only race where you'll need a separate water bottle just to make it in and out of transition. A GPS might also be helpful.

A full suspension mountain bike may indeed not be a bad choice for this race. It would certainly help you negotiate the maze of bumps, ruts, potholes, cracks, and fissures that is the paved surface of Lake Shore Drive. The tight steering angles afforded by a mountain bike would also help you avoid the dozens of stationary and mobile obstacles along the two loops. Some of my favorite stationary obstacles included dozens of stray water bottles and nutrition bars, a full set of aero bars (eek), a broken bicycle seat (ouch), and what I can only assume and hope was a dead rat (yuck).

Some of my favorite mobile obstacles included a very big girl on a cruiser with way under inflated tires bopping up and down like Mary Poppins on a Sunday ride. From the "now I've seen it all file,"; dozens of rolling orange cones whipped-up like tumbleweeds by the 40-mph winds, pro wannabes who, whipped up by their egos, zipped in and out of bike traffic yelling at all to get out of their way, and massive waves, whipped up by the winds, that crashed onto LSD like surf rolling onto a Hawaiian beach.

The Run

The run course follows the lakeshore heading south from transition, around the Shedd Aquarium, to McCormick Place and back north to the finish on Columbus Drive. Once again your first challenge is to find your stuff in transition. Last year the balloon parrot marking my spot had long since freed itself and departed, leaving me wandering the transition like a lost child at Costco. Having found my running stuff and the run exit, I happily exited the transition (only later did I realize what a terrible mistake this really was—please see NTKS) and began the run.

As a slow Clydesdale, I hate the run. This is the part of the race some runners just love to really stick it to us big guys. They come bounding by us like they're crazed kangaroos on uppers on their way to a 30-minute 10k. The Chicago Triathlon has a lot of these run weasels. Last year I was prepared. Not only was it cool (a Godsend to us big runners), but I also had a bit of a secret. And no I did not pump my butt up with steroids or slurp human growth hormones like Jose Conseco at his annual physical. I had, however, lived and trained at 6,000 feet above sea level, which gave me the legs of a running god...all be it a somewhat chunky and long in the tooth running god. No matter, I still ran the flat, twisty and cool course in a PB making me forget all the crazy stuff from the rest of the race.

The Race Expo

This is a true must go expo, as it is the largest and most packed of any race as befits the size of the race. Actually, you really must go to pick up your race packet and get body marked. With your numbers in place, you get to enter that exclusive world of triathlon racer a full day or two before the race and show off to all your neighbors, friends, and family. You can think to yourself—*That's right Mr. Chubby neighbor. I may be cutting the grass today I'm doing it with the form and physique of a race ready triathlete.* Plus there's lots of free swag to be had at the expo and you get the added benefit of savoring the pre-race buzz without having to break a sweat.

NTKS (Need To Know Secrets)

- You have two choices to get to transition from the swim exit. This is about a half a mile run (I'm not kidding here). You can run on the broken concrete path in your bare feet or you can run in the grass, but the grass hides broken glass. The smart move: bring your running shoes and stash them at the swim exit. The time it takes to throw them on is well worth the beating your feet will endure from either the broken concrete or stashed glass.

- Transition bike placement—the smart move: rack your bike as close to the bike exit as possible. If you stashed your shoes by the swim exit you'll wear them to your bike (remember transition is huge), and you'll also avoid much running time in your bike shoes out to the bike exit. On the way back, you'll also avoid running very far in your biking shoes to your stuff.

- After the race the line to get back into transition to get your stuff is longer than the toilet lines. Getting your stuff out of transition can take hours. The smart move, while everybody is in a huge line (at the south "run" end of the transition area) to get their stuff, walk around to the bike exit (north of end of the transition area) and avoid the long wait.

- Parking your car. If you get to the race late you'll have a hard time parking your car. The smart move: get to the race early (transitions opens at 4:30 a.m.—-no whining, you are a triathlete after all) and you'll have plenty of free street parking just around the corner from the race. As an added bonus you won't have to wait in a long line to get into transition, plus you can rack your bike right by the bike exit.

- It may take hours for your wave start. The smart move: get lucky with your race start time or bring a good book, iPod or friends and be ready to enjoy the wait.

About the Author

Roman Mica is a Clydesdale amateur triathlete who lives and races in the Mecca of triathlon, Boulder, Colorado. His favorite race drink is brewed by the Boulder Brewery and his favorite nutrition supplement is made by Dairy Queen.

He enjoys long leisurely walks along the lake front.... not! Actually, he loves to train and compete in triathlons. When he's not swimming, biking or running, he spends as much time as possible with his family.

To read more of Roman's advice and comments about Everyman Triathlon, visit his website:
http://everymantriathlon.blogs.com

About the Editor

Heather Hummel Ramsey resides in Charlottesville, Virginia. After several years of teaching English and Reading and Writing Across the Curriculum at the high school level, Heather decided to follow her path as a writer. A graduate with High Distinction from the University of Virginia, Heather has finished her first novel, *Touch of a Feather*, and is presently working on her second novel, *Coffee with Middle*.

Heather is an active member of the International Women's Writing Guild, Charlottesville Writing Center, James River Writers, and the UVA Bachelor of Interdisciplinary Studies Alumni Board. When Heather is not writing, she can be found cycling or playing with her two dogs, Julie and Stephan.

Publisher Information:

PathBinder Publishing
Charlottesville, VA
Web: www.PathBinder.com
E-mail: heatherhummel@PathBinder.com
Snail-mail:
PathBinder Publishing, LLC
P.O. Box 302
Earlysville, VA 22936

Also Available from PathBinder Publishing:
See 'Ville Run: A Collection of Running Tales
The Story of Our Fruits and Vegetables

Printed in the United States
59814LVS00002B/104